The Cost and Quality of Community Residential Care

An Evaluation of the Services for Adults with Learning Disabilities

Norma V. Raynes, Ken Wright,
Alan Shiell and Catherine Pettipher

David Fulton Publishers
London

David Fulton Publishers Ltd
2 Barbon Close, London WC1N 3JX

First published in Great Britain by
David Fulton Publishers 1994

Note: The right of the authors to be identified as the authors of this work has been asserted by them in accordance with the Copyright, Designs and Patents Act 1988.

Copyright © Norma V. Raynes, Ken Wright, Alan Shiell and Catherine Pettipher

British Library Cataloguing in Publication Data

A catalogue record for this book is available from the British Library

ISBN 1-85346-319-1

All rights reserved. No part of this publication may be reproduced, stored in a retrieval system or transmitted, in any form, or by any means, electronic, mechanical, photocopying, recording or otherwise, without the prior permission of the publishers.

Designed by Almac Ltd., London
Typeset by RP Typesetters Ltd., Unit 13, 21 Wren Street, London WC1X 0HF.
Printed in Great Britain by The Cromwell Press, Melksham, Wiltshire.

Contents

Acknowledgements		iv
CHAPTER 1	Background and Methods	1
CHAPTER 2	Facilities: Management, Size and Function	27
CHAPTER 3	Intersectoral Comparisons of Environmental Quality	35
CHAPTER 4	Staffing	63
CHAPTER 5	Characteristics of People in Residential Care	76
CHAPTER 6	The Costs of Community Residential Provision	80
CHAPTER 7	Policy Implications	94
Bibliography		100
Index		105

Acknowledgements

The authors gratefully acknowledge the assistance given by the proprietors, staff, residents and finance managers in the collection of the data on costs, quality of care and staffing of the homes. Acknowledgement is also made to the Department of Health for funding the research project. The usual disclaimers apply. Thanks are again due to Paula Press at the Centre for Health Economics at the University of York for typing the manuscript.

Chapter 1

Background and Methods

Background

There is an immediate problem of terminology when writing about the subject of this book. As is evident from the title, we have used the term 'people with learning disabilities' as a description of the residents of the homes included in this project. Using this term will be acceptable to some readers, to others it will be unacceptable. Some will prefer the use of the term 'mental handicap' which was common before 'learning disabilities' was adopted as the official description by the Department of Health. Indeed, in the renowned All Wales Strategy, the term 'mental handicap' is still used. Many references to previous published work also contain this terminology. Some people prefer the term 'learning difficulties' but others might see this as a very restricted description of the conditions under discussion. The description 'mental retardation' is common in the publications from the World Health Organization. Generally, though, what we would hope to show is that our concern is not so much terminology as value systems. The subject matter of this book is about the principles and objectives of residential care for people with learning disabilities (mental handicap, learning difficulties) and a contribution to the debate which is not about negative or politically incorrect labels but positive qualities of the environment in which people live, the care provided and the life-style adopted.

The research was carried out against a continuing debate about the objectives and values of residential care. Over the last decade there has been an increasing body of opinion amongst researchers and practitioners that the care of people with learning disabilities should follow the following five major principles or values (O'Brien, 1987):

Community presence: the right to participate in the life of the local community using general rather than specific facilities;
Relationships: the right to experience valued relationships;

Choice: the right to make choices about the ways in which people live;

Competence: the right to experience a growing ability to engage in meaningful activities with any assistance that may be required;

Respect: the right to be valued as citizens in their own rights.

The practical implementation of these principles in residential care has been taken to mean that homes should be closely integrated into local communities and in many ways should be indistinguishable from other dwellings in the neighbourhood. For many advocates of these accomplishments the appropriate dwelling is 'ordinary' houses within the general domestic housing stock, not purpose-built, isolated, specialist and usually large houses. The argument has been that the provision of domestic-scale living accommodation is more likely to achieve the objectives specified above and that specialist accommodation is unlikely to achieve appropriate integration in local communities.

There have been several objections or obstacles to pursuing the provision of small, 'ordinary housing' models of residential care:

- residential homes built since the transition to community care are often large (ie, provide for 20 or more residents). It is argued that it would be difficult to close these in favour of smaller housing accommodation;

- it is difficult to locate people with learning disabilities within the general population because prejudices, fear or ignorance would raise objections from nearby households;

- people with learning disabilities may not wish to be located amongst the general population;

- suitable property is difficult to find and adapt if the residents have difficulties getting around a house;

- costs increase rapidly as the number of people accommodated is reduced.

Although some of these issues have been researched before 1988, there was considerable concern that there was very little evidence available on how the size, location and ownership of homes affected costs and/or the achievement of good quality care.

The transition to community care or the resettlement of people into the community out of the large, specialized hospitals was also an important backcloth to the research. A considerable debate had raged throughout the 1970s and 1980s as to whether community care was more cost-effective than hospital care (Wright and Haycox, 1985). Gradually, evidence emerged that community care was more expensive than hospital care but it was also more effective (Knapp *et al.*, 1992). However, the interesting question of the relationship between costs, size, ownership and location of different forms of residential care in the community was still very much unexplored. In addition, the growth in the number of homes provided in the private and voluntary sectors and its effects on costs and quality of care had not been examined. Between 1980 and 1990 the number of places in private residential homes for people with learning disabilities in England increased from 1,617 to 8,382 and from 15,808 to 33,162 in voluntary homes (Darton and Wright, 1993). Although there was some evidence from the residential care of elderly people that private providers may be more efficient than public providers (Judge *et al.*, 1986), very little analysis had been carried out in residential homes for people with learning disabilities.

The methodology for the research was explored in two previous background papers on costs (Shiell and Wright, 1987) and measures of quality (Raynes, 1988). It was recognized from the outset that no single measure of quality of care could be used to assess all the different objectives that the residential homes might attempt to achieve. Previous work (Raynes and Sumpton, 1987) had already identified several important dimensions to the quality of care including: the physical characteristics of the home, its location, age, ownership, facilities and general state of cleanliness and repair; the activities provided or arranged for residents either in the home or in the community; the degree of choice or control residents had over their daily living routines, diet, dress, relationships, friendships and time; the experience, qualifications and attitude of owners, managers and staff to residents. It was also realized that the age, abilities, family networks, state of health and medical requirements of residents might affect the activities they enjoyed, the staff and services they needed and the costs they incurred. Data on all these factors were collected and analysed as part of the research, which is reported in the following chapters. The management, size and functions of the homes are reported in Chapter 2. An analysis of the intersectoral comparisons of environmental quality is set out in

Chapter 3. Chapter 4 is devoted to the issue of staffing the homes. The characteristics of residents are described in Chapter 5 and the relationships between costs, size, control, ownership and quality of care are analysed in Chapter 6. A summing-up of findings and a discussion of their policy implications are presented in Chapter 7.

Introduction to the Survey

This book presents the results of a four year study designed to investigate and explain the costs and quality of community residential services for adults with learning disabilities. The first two years of the work were concerned with costing different services for people with learning disabilities and developing the research proposal for the cost and quality project. Fieldwork for the project was carried out between April 1988 and May 1989.

The aims of the research were fourfold:

1. To assess and measure various dimensions of the quality of service being provided in a sample of staffed community residential facilities accommodating people with learning disabilities.
2. To measure the economic costs associated with these services.
3. To explain variations in the quality of service provision.
4. To explain variations in the costs of care.

Sample

Planned sample

The sample consisted of 200 staffed facilities providing residential accommodation for adults with learning disabilities. Selection of the facilities was dependent upon size and administering agency. Fifty facilities in each of the size categories 1-4, 5-8, 9-18 and 19-28 were drawn at random from the Department of Health's Gazetteers (DHSS, 1986; 1987a; 1987b). The sample was designed to reflect the proportion of residential facilities in England, excluding the London Boroughs, run by each type of agency. (Some District Health Authorities which straddled a Greater London authority such as Kingston and Esher, have been included.) The agencies covered were Local Authority Social Service Departments, District Health

Authorities and private and voluntary agencies (see Table 1.1). The Social Services and Health Authority facilities were located in 39 Local Authorities and 33 Health Authorities, respectively. The private and voluntary facilities were located in 25 Local Authorities and 21 Local Authorities, respectively.

All of the facilities selected were community residences providing accommodation for adults only or a mixture of adults and juniors. According to the DHSS Statistical Unit for Local Authorities, the minimum age for an adult is 16 years. To be included in the sample, facilities had to be either permanently staffed or staffed for at least part of the time during the day.

Table 1.1 Number of facilities selected by agency type and size category

Type of Agency	Size (no. of places)				
	1-4	5-8	9-18	19-28	TOTAL
Local Authority	9	7	13	36	65
Health Authority	17	12	8	6	43
Private Sector	17	20	19	3	59
Voluntary Sector	7	11	10	5	33
TOTAL	50	50	50	50	200

Achieved sample

In all, 150 facilities were visited. On arrival some of the facilities had more places than expected.

Table 1.2 Number of facilities visited by agency type and size category

Type of Agency	Size (no. of places)						
	1-4	5-8	9-18	19-28	29+	No info	TOTAL
Local Authority	10	6	9	33	1	0	59
Health Authority	16	11	7	7	0	0	41
Private Sector	0	6	15	3	0	0	24
Voluntary Sector	5	8	11	1	0	1	26
TOTAL	31	31	42	44	1	1	150

In the achieved sample, the Local Authority facilities were located in 36 Local Authorities; the Health Authority facilities were located in 31 Health Authorities, and the private and voluntary facilities were located in 24 and 26 Local Authorities respectively.

Table 1.3 Achieved sample: mean number of places, standard deviation and range for the sample in each agency

Agency	Mean	Standard Deviation	Range	N
Local Authority	17.5	9.0	2-31	59
Health Authority	9.3	7.4	2-24	41
Private Sector	12.8	4.9	6-24	24
Voluntary Sector	9.5	5.5	3-27	26
TOTAL	13.1	8.3	2031	150

Process of Acces to the Facility

To gain access to the Local Authority and Health Authority facilities we initially approached the agency responsible for the facility. Where agreement was obtained, the facility staff were written to directly, asking for their consent and that of the residents to a visit by a research team member. For private and voluntary facilities we wrote directly to the facility asking for permission to visit. In all, four research staff took part in the fieldwork, although the majority of visits were carried out by three research members.

During the course of access, the original sample we had drawn had to be modified and substitutes were found for certain facilities. In total, 44 substitutes had to be made covering 37 facilities. Substitutes were randomly drawn from the original data-pool, given the constraints of an appropriate agency and size category to match the facility being replaced.

Some facilities had to be dropped from the sample. These included those who refused and those who did not respond to our efforts to contact them. Definitions for each are given below.

- Refusals

    These include those who wrote back saying that they refused to participate in the study.

- Non-responders

    These include those facilities who failed to reply after one initial contact letter and three follow-up letters.

- Substitutes

    a) those that turned out to have changed their function since the latest gazetteer was published so as not to come within our remit

    b) those who were found to have been wrongly classified by the gazetteer and which did not come within our remit

    (examples of substitutes include those facilities found to be registered for the mentally ill only, those registered for children and those registered for short-stay people)

    c) those facilities that were 'not known' at the address specified in the gazetteer.

Data Sources

Establishment questionnaire

The establishment questionnaire consisted of two parts which together comprised the sections shown in Figure 1.1.

Figure 1.1 The establishment questionnaire

```
PART 1

    1. Identification of facility
    2. Staffing
    3. Residents
    4. Safety

PART 2

    5. Physical environment
    6. Observations
```

The first part of this questionnaire took the form of a structured interview with the officer in charge or the owner of the facility.

Occasionally other members of staff of the facility were present. The interview lasted between one and a half and two hours.

The second part consisted of a checklist which had to be completed by means of observation. The officer in charge or owner was asked whether it would be possible to have a look at each room in the facility, including the residents' bedrooms, given their permission. Usually the research member was taken round the facility by one of the residents.

Part of the checklist involved observation at mealtimes. This was completed only if it was mutually convenient for the research members to stay and have a meal with the residents.

Client questionnaire

During the course of the site visit the researcher left client questionnaires to be filled in on behalf of the client by a key worker or someone who knew the client well. A questionnaire was left for each long-stay client only (excluding any children). The main sections comprising the client questionnaire are shown in Figure 1.2.

Figure 1.2 The client questionnaire

---
1. General information (demographic)
2. Health and Social Services
3. Levels of dependency
4. Services provided and needed for clients
5. Contacts with people and places outside
6. Client's daily life
7. Opportunities for clients to make choices
8. National development team assessment form
9. Future needs

Staff questionnaire

Whilst at the facility, the researchers also left self-administered questionnaires for each member of staff. Each questionnaire was accompanied by a covering letter which explained the purpose of the visit, and a stamped addressed envelope. Details of the contents of the questionnaire are shown in Figure 1.3.

Figure 1.3 The staff questionnaire

> Questions were included on:
>
> 1. Experience of working with people with learning disabilities
> 2. Job title
> 3. Staff morale and job satisfaction
> 4. Staff attitudes to people with learning disabilities
> 5. Satisfaction with communication with other staff

Central questionnaire

This was sent to a named contact in the statutory agencies requesting details of annual revenue costs, capital values of facilities, resident admissions and staff turnover. Details of the costs of voluntary facilities were obtained either from the officer in charge or from a named treasurer on the management committee. Estimates of the costs of private sector facilities were based on the average charge. Details of charges were obtained from proprietors.

Response Rate

Facilities

Table 1.4 shows the number of facilities which agreed to participate in the study and were visited by a member of the study team.

Table 1.4 Completion rate and sample size, within agency

Agency	Completion Rate (%)	No. of Facilities
Local Authority	91	59
Health Authority	95	41
Private Sector	41	24
Voluntary Sector	79	26
Overall	75	150

Thus, 150 out of an original sample of 200 facilities were visited. Table 1.5 shows a breakdown of the reasons for not visiting the remaining 50 facilities. Note, one completed questionnaire for a Local Authority facility was lost and therefore data for some items are reported for 149 homes.

Table 1.5 Reasons why facilities were not visited

Agency	Number of Facilities		
	Refused	Non-response	Misclassified and Not Replaced
Local Authority	6	–	–
Health Authority	1	–	1
Private Sector	20	13	2
Voluntary Sector	5	2	–
Overall	32	15	3

Client questionnaires

Table 1.6 shows the response rate to the client questionnaire.

Table 1.6 Response rate for client questionnaire and sample size, within agency

Agency	Response Rate (%)	No. Returned
Local Authority	81	743
Health Authority	75	235
Private Sector	77	217
Voluntary Sector	79	173
Overall	79	1368

Staff questionnaire

Table 1.7 shows the response rate to the staff questionnaire.

Table 1.7 Response rate for staff questionnaire and sample size, within agency

Agency	Response Rate (%)	No. Returned
Local Authority	59	472
Health Authority	53	269
Private Sector	56	144
Voluntary Sector	58	121
Overall	57	1006

Measures Contained in the Questionnaire

Contained within the establishment, client and staff questionnaire were several scales.

Quality instruments

Index of Participation in Domestic Life (IPDL)

This measure is designed to identify the extent to which residents are given opportunities to participate in everyday domestic tasks. Developed by Raynes and Sumpton (1986), it contains 13 items (see Figure 1.4) each rated on a three-point scale. Lower scores reflect maximum opportunity to carry out the domestic task, ie, clients do the task alone or with other peers. Item scores are summed to give an overall index score ranging from 13-39. The internal reliability of the scale, using Cronbach Alpha has been reported as 0.90 (Raynes and Sumpton, 1986). We obtained a Cronbach Alpha coefficient of 0.93 with the data we collected. This scale is in the client's questionnaire in the section on client's daily life.

Figure 1.4 Participation in domestic life

---
1. Shopping for food
2. Preparing meals
3. Setting table
4. Serving meals
5. Washing up
6. Cleaning kitchen
7. Cleaning living and dining room
8. Cleaning own bedroom
9. Cleaning bathroom and toilet
10. Shopping for supplies
11. Doing own washing
12. Doing own ironing
13. Looking after garden

Index of Adult Autonomy (IAA)

The Index of Adult Autonomy was designed by Raynes and Sumpton (1986) to assess the extent to which adults are given opportunities to make decisions about various aspects of their daily lives.

It contains 11 items which cover aspects of daily life and the opportunity residents have to participate in making decisions about them (see Figure 1.5).

Figure 1.5 Index of Adult Autonomy

---

1. Does the client have a bank, post office or building society account?
2. How much do you let this client decide to spend for him/herself?
3. Does this client have a front door key or access to one?
4. Do you let this client go out into the community to meet friends?
5. Do you let this client have access to a pay phone?
6. If this client goes out in the evening does he/she have to be back by a set time?
7. Do you let this client choose what clothes he/she wears each day?
8. Do you let this client choose the way he/she has his/her hair?
9. Does this client have to be in bed by a set time at night?
10. Do you let this client use public transport by him/herself?
11. Do you let this client shop for his/her own clothes, choosing what he/she wants to buy?

Each item is scored on a three-point scale and scores are summed to provide an index score. Higher scores indicate a greater opportunity to participate in decision making. The internal reliability of the Index, as shown by the Cronbach Alpha coefficient, has been reported as 0.77 (Raynes and Sumpton, 1986). Using our data we obtained a Cronbach Alpha coefficient of 0.82.

Choice-making Scale (CMS)

The Choice-making Scale developed by Conroy and Feinstein (1986) is used in the client questionnaire in section 7, 'Making Choices'. It contains six sections which together include 24 items (see Figure 1.6).

Figure 1.6 Choice-making Scales

FOOD
   1. What foods to buy for the home when shopping
   2. What to have for the main meal
   3. What to eat (and ignore) from plate
   4. Desserts and snacks
   5. Choosing cafes

HOUSE, ROOM
   6. Decorations in own room
   7. Choosing to be alone
   8. Type of personal hygiene articles
   9. Setting house or room temperature for personal comfort

CLOTHES
   10. What clothes to buy
   11. What clothes to wear (including both weekdays and weekends)
   12. What to wear to bed

SLEEPING AND WAKING
   13. When to go to bed on weekdays
   14. When to go to bed on weekends
   15. When to get up on weekends
   16. Taking naps in evenings and on weekends
   17. Time and frequency of bathing or showering

RECREATION
   18. Choice of outings, field trips
   19. What to watch on TV
   20. Visiting with friends

OTHER
   21. What to buy or do with personal money
   22. Choice about taking medications (how, with what, when)
   23. How and when to express affection for others
   24. 'Minor vices' – use of tobacco, alcohol, caffeine, etc.

The scale was developed to estimate the extent to which staff encouraged residents' efforts to make choices.

Each item is rated on a four-point scale ranging from 'no opportunities for making choices' to 'yes, opportunities for making choices all of the time'. Scale scores range from 24 to 96; the higher the score, the more opportunity the client is given for making choices. With our data we obtained a reliability coefficient of 0.96, using Cronbach's Alpha.

Index of Community Involvement (ICI)

The Index of Community Involvement (Raynes and Sumpton, 1986) consists of 15 items. Fourteen of these ascertain whether clients have used specified facilities in the community within the past four weeks. The fifteenth item relates to going on holiday within the previous 12 months (see Figure 1.7).

Figure 1.7 Index of Community Involvement

1. Hairdresser
2. Friends in for meal
3. Guest to stay
4. Overnight visit to family or friends
5. Shopping
6. Pub
7. Cinema
8. Restaurant or cafe
9. Place of worship
10. Sports events, eg, swimming, football match
11. Club
12. Theatre
13. Bus
14. Bank
15. Holiday in the past 12 months

For each item the percentage of residents in the facility who have been to the amenity in the previous four weeks is recorded. These are then converted to a score ranging from 0 to 4 as follows:

Score	Percentage of residents
0	0 – 19
1	20 – 39
2	40 – 59
3	60 – 79
4	80 – 100

Scale scores range from 0 to 60 with higher scores reflecting high involvement with the community. Using the present data we obtained a Cronbach Alpha coefficient of 0.70.

Family and Friend Contact Measures

These are located in the client questionnaire in the section 'Contact with people and places outside'. A scale of family contact was constructed by combining the responses to each of three items relating to contact with client's families (see Figure 1.8). Each item was rated on a four-point scale relating to frequency of visits: weekly, monthly, less often and never. Scale scores range from 3 to 12; the lower the score the greater the family contact. We obtained a measure of internal reliability using Cronbach's Alpha coefficient, of 0.74.

Figure 1.8 Contact with family

---
1. How often do family members visit
2. How often do family members contact client other than by visits
3. How often does this client go home

A similar four-point scale was constructed to measure the extent of contact with friends. In this case, the responses to two items were combined, producing a scale ranging from 2 to 8 (see Figure 1.9). As with the family contact scale, the lower scores indicate a greater amount of contact with friends. The Cronbach Alpha coefficient we obtained was 0.70.

Figure 1.9 Contact with friends

---
1. How often do the client's friends visit this residence
2. How often does the client visit his/her friends

Plans for Clients Measure

To obtain a measure of the extent to which written plans existed for clients a scale containing eight items was constructed. We asked whether plans were available in the areas shown in Figure 1.10.

Figure 1.10 Plans for clients

---
1. Employment needs
2. Medical needs
3. Family contact needs
4. Residential care needs
5. Emotional need
6. Self-help skills, eg, dressing and undressing
7. Community skills, eg, shopping, literacy and numeracy
8. Recreational skills

'Yes' responses were coded 1 and 'No' responses were coded 2, giving a scale score range of 8 to 16. The lower the score, the more likely there are to be written plans in various areas. This scale is in the section 'Services provided and needed for clients' in the client questionnaire. The internal reliability of the scale using the present data shows a Cronbach Alpha coefficient of 0.84.

Indexes relating to the home as a whole

Group Homes Management Scale (GHMS)

This scale, developed by Pratt *et al.* (1979), measures the extent to which different practices are resident-orientated, flexible and individually based. It contains ten items (see Figure 1.11).

Figure 1.11 Group Homes Management Scale

---
1. Do the residents always get up at weekends at the same time as they do during the week
2. Is breakfast served at the same time at weekends as it is during the week
3. Is the evening meal served at the same time at weekends as it is during the week
---

> 4. Do residents go to bed at the same time at weekends as they do during the week
> 5. How are meals planned at the residence
> 6. Who shops for groceries
> 7. Who shops for clothing and personal articles
> 8. How is banking handled
> 9. How are the household chores allocated
> 10. Who organizes parties at the residence

Each item is rated on a four-point scale with total scores ranging from 0 to 30. Higher scores indicate greater flexibility within the home. The Cronbach Alpha coefficient obtained by Pratt *et al.* (1979) showed the scale to be of high internal reliability (alpha = 0.89). We obtained a similar coefficient (alpha = 0.84).

Staff Autonomy Scale

The Staff Autonomy Scale, located in the establishment questionnaire, is designed to assess the extent of autonomy that the person in charge of the home has about daily events (Raynes *et al.*, 1977). The scale contains 11 items (see Figure 1.12) which are rated on a three-point scale with higher scores indicating more control over decision making.

Figure 1.12 Staff Autonomy Scale

> Who is responsible for deciding:
>
> 1. What time the residents get up
> 2. What time the residents go to bed
> 3. The admission of a resident
> 4. The discharge of a resident
> 5. When a resident can go on home leave or away
> 6. Who should come to work in the residence
> 7. Who should be dismissed from the residence
> 8. What days off staff should have
> 9. When staff should take their annual leave or other holidays
> 10. The planning of individual programmes for residents
> 11. The use of transport for the resident's needs.

Using our data, we obtained a Cronbach Alpha reliability coefficient of 0.64.

Environmental Quality Scale

This scale, located in the section on physical quality, aims to provide an overall rating of the pleasantness of the residence and the neighbourhood in which the home is located. Developed by Seltzer (1981) and subsequently modified by Temple University (see Raynes, 1988), it consists of six items each of which is rated by means of observation on a four-point scale (see Figure 1.13).

Figure 1.13 Environmental Quality Scale

---
1. As a neighbourhood, how does the area around the site look
2. How attractive are the site grounds
3. How attractive are the site buildings
4. Variation in design of resident's rooms
5. Individuality of resident's rooms
6. Overall physical pleasantness of the facility

The range of scores is 0 to 18 with high scores representing pleasant and attractive facilities in which high levels of individuality and variation are shown. Using our data, the internal reliability of the scale as shown by Cronbach Alpha was 0.64.

Room Rating Scale

This measure, developed by Conroy and Bradley (1985) assesses each type of room in the home. It covers five aspects of the room: its orderliness, its cleanliness, the condition of the furniture in it, its lightness and its freshness (see Figure 1.14).

Figure 1.14 Room Rating Scale

---
1. Orderliness/clutter
2. Cleanliness of walls and floors (or carpets)
3. Condition of furniture
4. Window areas
5. Odours

Each aspect is rated on a four-point scale giving a scale score ranging from 0 to 15. Higher scores represent better environmental quality, that is rooms which are neat and well maintained, airy and fresh smelling. This scale can be found in section 5, on 'Physical quality' in the establishment questionnaire. An internal reliability of the scale using the data we collected gives a Cronbach Alpha coefficient of 0.67.

Mealtime Scale

This scale was constructed in order to measure the extent of homeliness at mealtimes. It contains four items (see Figure 1.15), each of which is rated on a three-point scale.

Figure 1.15 Mealtime Scale

---
1. How are the tables set for the meal
2. Do staff and clients/residents talk to each other during the meal
3. Do the clients/residents wait before meals
4. Do the clients/residents wait after meals

Scale scores range from 0 to 8, the higher score reflecting the more homely environment. A reliability analysis carried out on the data we obtained gives a Cronbach Alpha coefficient of 0.67.

Indexes relating to staff satisfaction, communication and attitudes -

Staff Satisfaction

The measure used to assess staff satisfaction was developed by Willcocks *et al.* (1987). Staff were required to rate their satisfaction with each of the 16 items shown in Figure 1.16 according to a seven-point rating scale ranging from extremely satisfied to extremely dissatisfied.

Figure 1.16 Staff satisfaction

---
1. The physical working conditions
2. The freedom to choose their own method of working
3. Fellow workers
4. The recognition they got for their work
5. Immediate superiors

> 6. The amount of responsibility staff are given
> 7. The rate of pay
> 8. The opportunity to use their ability
> 9. Relations between bosses and workers in residential care
> 10. Chances of promotion
> 11. The way the facility is managed
> 12. The attention paid to suggestions staff make
> 13. Hours of work
> 14. The amount of variety
> 15. Job security
> 16. The job as a whole

Scale scores range from 0 to 96; the higher the score the more satisfied the person is with aspects of the job. Using our data we obtained a measure of internal reliability of Cronbach Alpha = 0.91.

Staff Attitudes to People with a Mental Handicap

To measure staff attitudes, a questionnaire developed by Allen *et al.* (1985) was used. This measure consists of eight items with a five-point scale ranging from agree to disagree. Four items in the scale are scored in reverse order. Figure 1.17 shows the statements which staff were asked to rate.

Figure 1.17 Staff attitudes

> 1. Mentally handicapped residents appreciate attractive surroundings
> 2. Therapy can achieve little with severely handicapped residents
> 3. Sexually active residents should be sterilized
> 4. Residents can respond to care
> 5. Residents should not be treated like young children
> 6. Most residents will never know right from wrong
> 7. Little can be done to help severely handicapped residents to improve
> 8. Residents can often lead a life which is as valuable as anyone else's

Communication Measure

Two measures of satisfaction with communication were constructed.

The first, 'Communication with line managers', contained three items (see Figure 1.18) which had to be rated on a five-point scale ranging from 'very unsatisfactory' to 'very satisfactory'. Thus, scale scores range from 3 to 15 with higher scores indicating higher satisfaction with opportunities for communication. With the present data, we obtained a reliability coefficient of 0.85 using Cronbach's Alpha.

Figure 1.18 Communication Scale

1. The residents
2. The job to be done and ways to do it
3. Other work-related matters, for example, hours of work or pay

The second measure, 'Communication with colleagues', consists of the same items and rating scale but explores how satisfied staff were with the opportunities they had to discuss aspects of their work with their immediate colleagues. Again, scale scores range from 3 to 15 with the higher the score the greater the degree of satisfaction. Using the Cronbach Alpha coefficient we obtained a measure of internal reliability of 0.87.

Costs

The method used to estimate the costs of residential services was described in an earlier paper (Shiell and Wright, 1987). Briefly, it involved adjusting the accounted expenditure of each facility to net out the costs of services provided to people who were not resident and to add in the costs of services used by the residents but not accounted to the residential facility. The latter included the costs of additional day services and the cost of domiciliary health and personal social services.

Estimates of the costs of private sector facilities have been based on the average charge levied in each home rather than accounted expenditure. This was done primarily for pragmatic reasons though the practice does have some theoretical justification. The residual which accrues to the proprietor after running costs have been met from fee-income represents a return to the owner for the use of capital and the bearing of risk, as well as payment for time the owner puts in either to the care of residents or to the management of the home. So long as there is competition between the providers of residential homes, then market forces should ensure that the return to owners is economically fair and equal in value to the marginal owners' input.

The principal resources used in providing residential care are staff, non-staff recurrent items (food, energy costs, etc.), day services, domiciliary health services, volunteers and capital. The specific methods used to cost each resource are outlined below.

Staff

Wherever possible, salary costs have been taken from facility accounts. The cost of staff hours provided in support of residents in other related facilities (group homes, for example) has been subtracted. Similarly, the cost of any input from staff based in other facilities provided in support of residents included in the study has been added. The cost of residential staff who provide a peripatetic service to homes has been calculated by multiplying the average number of hours of staff time by the mid-points of appropriate salary scales.

Non-staff recurrent costs

Estimates of the expenditure on provisions, energy costs, establishment expenses, etc. have also been taken from the accounts of facilities. In facilities where the residents are responsible for the purchase of such recurrent items out of their social security entitlements, household budgets have been used instead. In all cases, known costs of management and central administration have been excluded to facilitate comparison with facilities where such information is unavailable.

Day services

Regular attendance at Local Authority day centres has been costed using published average costs (CIPFA, 1988a). Similarly, the cost of full-time adults and special education has been costed at average costs per pupil (CIPFA, 1988b).

Domiciliary health services

Information on the use of a number of health and personal social services was used to cost this additional input. Costs of domiciliary services have been calculated by multiplying the number of consultations for each resident in a facility by an estimate of their average duration, valued at rates taken from the PSSRU 'Care in the Community' development project (Knapp *et al.*, 1992). Hospital visits and stays have been costed at average costs per attendance or inpatient days. To avoid double counting, notional costs for such services appearing in the accounts of facilities have been subtracted.

Volunteers

Overall, the use of volunteers (including people employed on community or employment training schemes) was not substantial, though it was important in one or two facilities. Where volunteers were used, the officers in charge generally regarded their input as making a significant contribution to the service provided. The services of volunteers have therefore been costed by using the wage rates of equivalent unskilled staff.

Capital

Information on the capital value of properties in which residential services were provided was not generally available. Fortunately, the NHS had recently undertaken an extensive review of the value of its estate and access to the results of this survey was granted to the study team. Where information on the capital value of other facilities was not available, estimates were compiled in one of two ways. For domestic-scale properties, proxy values were taken with reference to the local housing market. Values of larger properties and all purpose-built facilities were estimated from construction-cost guidance as used by quantity surveyors. Once estimated, the capital value was transformed into an annual equivalent sum by a simple arithmetic process similar to calculating mortgage repayments. The resulting estimates are necessarily crude approximations, though any distortion caused by error should be slight because capital costs comprise only about 10 per cent of recurrent expenditure once the capital value is expressed in annual equivalent terms.

The aim of the costing has been to compile an estimate of the resource or economic costs of residential services, including the use of domiciliary health services and day services. The systematic and comprehensive nature of the costing facilitates comparisons of the costs of care in different residential settings.

Reliability

The sample

It can be seen from Table 1.4 that the completion rate for facilities in the private sector was only 41 per cent. Thus, in order to establish whether the facilities we visited were representative of the private sector, we carried out a reliability study. This aimed to investigate whether there were any significant differences between the characteristics of facilities which participated in the study and those which did not.

To do this we carried out a series of telephone interviews with the registration officers concerned with all 59 private facilities. Initially we contacted the appropriate directors of Social Services to gain permission to approach the registration officers and to confirm that the enquiry was confidential. A research assistant then telephoned each registration officer and asked the questions shown in Figure 1.19.

Figure 1.19 Questions asked of registration officers

1. Do the owners have any professional training
2. What is the date of registration for learning disabilities places
3. How many places is it registered for
4. How many places are for short-stay or respite care
5. How many people are currently resident
6. Is the facility purpose-built, an ordinary house or some other kind of building
7. How many bedrooms are there
8. How many single bedrooms are there
9. What kind of area is it located in
10. What fees are charged per person per week
11. How many residents use the local ATC/SEC daily
12. Are any services for disabled people close by the facility
13. How many whole-time equivalent staff are there

The items were selected from the establishment questionnaire and were seen as providing information on the basic characteristics of the facility.

To test whether there were any significant differences between visited and non-visited facilities, t-tests and chi-square tests were carried out as appropriate. The only comparison that was significant was the area in which the facility was located (chi-square – 9.0, df 3, p<0.05). This indicated a difference between visited and non-visited facilities regarding whether the location was urban, suburban, a rural village or classed as rural isolated. Table 1.8 shows details of the type of areas in which the facilities were located.

Table 1.8 Type of area for facilities in visited and non-visited samples (%)

	Visited	Not Visited
Urban	25	34
Suburban	42	26
Rural Village	29	–
Rural Isolated	4	3
Missing	–	37

Facilities which were not visited were more likely to be in urban areas and less likely to be in suburban areas and rural villages than those visited.

Since there were no significant differences on any other comparisons, it suggests there is no substantial difference in basic characteristics of those facilities which participated and those which did not. However, the registration officers did have some difficulties in obtaining the information, particularly from homes which did not participate in the study (see Table 1.9). The registration officers had no information about at least one-third of the homes not visited by the team and for some items, this proportion rose to a half (Raynes, 1990). Therefore, some doubt about the representativeness of the private sector facilities which participated in the study still remains.

Table 1.9 Percentage of facilities for which information was not available from registration officers

Area on which Information was Requested Research Team	Visited by Research Team	Not Visited
1. Do the owners have any professional training	21	40
2. What is date of registration for learning disabilities places	17	32
3. How many places is it registered for	–	34
4. How many places are for short-stay or respite care	46	49

5. How many people are currently resident	13	40
6. Is the facility purpose-built, an ordinary house or some other kind of building	0	34
7. How many bedrooms are there	8	43
8. How many single bedrooms are there	8	46
9. What kind of area is it located in	–	37
10. What fees are charged per person per week	17	43
11. How many residents use the local ATC/SEC daily	38	54
12. Are any services for disabled people close by the facility	8	40
13. How many whole-time equivalent staff are there	50	49

Establishment questionnaire: reliability between interviewers

In order to check on the agreement between interviewers as to the coding of the interviewee's responses for the establishment questionnaire, a reliability study was carried out. A different pair of interviewers visited three different homes. At each home, both research members recorded the responses of the officer in charge. One research member conducted the interview whilst the other sat quietly in the background and recorded the responses. The results show that, on average, interviewers agreed on 88 per cent of the items.

Coding reliability

The establishment questionnaire was coded prior to being put online by three different people. As a check on the agreement between coders, a reliability study was carried out. Ten per cent of each person's questionnaires were re-coded by a different person. The study showed that, overall, the agreement between coders was very high. For the first part of the establishment questionnaire – the structured interview, agreement was 98 per cent, while for the observation checklist, in the second part of the questionnaire, agreement was 99 per cent. Thus, coding reliability can be said to be highly satisfactory.

Chapter 2

Facilities: Management, Size and Function

Summary

- In 83 per cent of facilities, a single agency is responsible for both staffing and material resources. The greatest diversity of management arrangements is in the voluntary sector.

- Problems in coordinating the resources needed to provide a quality service were as likely to arise in single-agency homes as in multi-agency ones.

- Facilities ranged in size from 2 to 31 places; mean size was 13.1 places. Health Authority and voluntary sector facilities tended to be the smallest, and Local Authority facilities the biggest.

- Over one-half of Local Authority facilities and one-quarter of Health Authority facilities are subdivided internally to provide smaller-group living spaces.

- Facilities serve a wide range of functions in addition to providing continuing residential accommodation and care.

Introduction

In this chapter, the two variables used to stratify the sample – management agency and size – are considered in more detail. The functions served by the residential facilities are also examined to shed light upon the role each facility was expected to play by the agency responsible for its provision.

Management Agency

Principal management agency was self-defined according to the entry in the relevant DHSS gazetteer. In practice, a variety of agencies may be involved in the provision of residential services centred on a particular facility. Table 2.1 shows the number of facilities grouped according to the agency principally responsible for two key resources: staffing and capital. In 83 per cent of the facilities, a single agency is responsible for providing both key resources (funding is not considered here, so, for example, a council house is classified under Local Authority Housing Department regardless of the ultimate source of rental payments). In all but two of the facilities in which this was not the case, responsibility for staff determined the management agency. In these, the property was formally rented (or use otherwise secured) from council housing departments or housing associations. One Health Authority facility was situated in the principal staff member's own home and operated as a shared-living scheme. Private facilities were all single-agency and in all but one case the property was owned or under mortgage to the registered proprietors. In the one exception, the proprietor rented from a specialist property-letting company.

Table 2.1 Number of facilities by management of principal resource

Staff	Property					TOTAL
	LASSD	LA Housing Dept	HA	Private	Vol	
Local Authority	49	7	0	0	4	60
Health Authority	0	8	28	1	5	42
Private Sector	0	0	0	24	0	24
Voluntary Sector	1	1	2	2	18	24
TOTAL	50	16	30	27	27	150

The greatest diversity was amongst the facilities designated in the gazetteer as voluntary. Four of the 26 voluntary facilities were located in property rented from statutory agencies and one was rented privately at a fair rent. One further facility, classified here as being located in private property, operated as a group-living scheme. Three voluntary facilities were located in properties rented from housing associations and, in each case, there were close organizational links between the two voluntary agencies. This was in contrast to Health and Local Authority facilities rented from housing associations where the respective agencies tended to be organizationally distinct from one another.

In only two facilities did responsibility for staff not determine the management agency. Both of these were classified in the gazetteer as voluntary and both were located in properties managed by housing associations, though in one, staff were seconded from Social Services (with partial reimbursement of costs) and in the other, the sole staff member was employed by the Health Authority.

Finally, it should be noted that in five of the 28 facilities classified here as being single-agency Health Authority, residents paid rent for their accommodation. In two of these, a voluntary organization administered the non-staff revenue expenditure out of social security payments.

Facilities which were wrongly classified in the gazetteer were replaced in our sample (see Chapter 1). This may understate the extent of multiple-agency involvement in the provision of residential services because the capacity for mis-classification is obviously higher where more than one agency is involved in the delivery of care. The number of agencies involved in any one facility may also be expected to increase as one considers responsibility for resources other than staffing and premises (day services, for example) and as a result of policy initiatives to encourage greater involvement of the independent sector in the future. Classification of facilities according to management agency will become more complex as the number of agencies involved in the delivery of services to the residents of facilities increase and this will have implications for research concerned with identifying intersectoral differences in the provision of services.

A common source of complaint from the people in charge of residential facilities was the difficulty in organizing the material requirements necessary to provide a service of the quality desired. Important elements, such as redecorating a room or replacing old items of furniture, might be under the control of an outside works manager or housing agency who may not share the philosophy of care or the priorities of staff and residents. However, these problems were as likely to arise in single-agency facilities where responsibility for such matters might be in a different department or sector of the same agency as in facilities with more complex multi-agency management arrangements. The problem is more one of coordinating the necessary resources rather than coordinating the agencies. Difficulties were reportedly fewer where budgets were devolved to facility managers, allowing the staff to determine their own spending priorities.

Size of Facilities

The size of the facilities is defined in terms of the total number of residential places available on the day each facility was visited, though the sample was originally stratified according to the number of available places reported in the respective gazetteers. The time-lag between the submission of information to the Department for inclusion in the gazetteer and our visit to each facility led to surprisingly few discrepancies in the reported size of facilities. Four facilities (two private and two voluntary) had more places than they were originally registered for, though the additional numbers were small (three or fewer extra places). One voluntary facility had one less place. Finally, two large Local Authority hostels, one of which was scheduled for closure, and one Health Authority hostel, were running down the number of places by not replacing residents who left and so, in each case, there was a shortfall in the number of places actually encountered.

The facilities ranged in size from 2 to 31 places with a mean size of 13.1 places. Inter-authority variations in size of facility (see Table 2.2) reflect the differences in the type of building in which each facility was located. Local Authority facilities tended to be in purpose-built hostels and Health Authority facilities in ordinary housing, while the independent sector make extensive use of very large or out of the ordinary housing.

Table 2.2 Size of facilities

Agency	Mean No. of Places	s.d.
Local Authority	17.5	9.0
Health Authority	9.3	7.4
Private Sector	12.8	4.9
Voluntary Sector	9.5	5.5
All Facilities	13.1	8.3

Comparisons of size are distorted slightly by differences in definition which affect out sample base. Health Authority community units are distinguished from hospitals by having fewer than 30 beds. In practice, while there are no facilities with more than 30 beds included in the 'community' returns, there are a number of facilities of less than 30 in the 'hospital' gazetteer. In contrast, *all* Local

Authority units are defined as being in the community, including those with more than 30 places. Our sample includes two such facilities. Furthermore, while there is no upper limit on the size of private or voluntary sector facilities, the sample had to be drawn from *registered* homes as no central record exists of unregistered facilities. This provides an effective lower limit on size as registration was only required for homes with four or more places, at the time the sample was drawn.

The effective size of the living units is also a function of the design of the residential facilities. For example, a 24-place facility might be a single large hostel, a large hostel subdivided internally to provide a number of semi-autonomous sub-units, or a campus arrangement of three neighbouring bungalows, each of which is entirely self-contained. In total, 42 facilities were subdivided internally to provide smaller effective living spaces. Only two of these were not provided by the statutory sector. Internal subdivision results in the reduction of the effective mean size of living units to 8.9 places (see Table 2.3) but it should be noted that in a few instances subdivision meant using ex-staff accommodation to provide a semblance of independent living to one or two residents only. In these facilities, the bulk of residents are still living in relatively large groups.

Such arrangements are often an attempt to capture the advantages of smallness whilst retaining the economies of scale usually present in larger units. The success of this strategy is discussed further in Chapter 6. For the moment, size of facility will continue to be regarded as the total number of places available irrespective of the internal organization of facilities.

Table 2.3 Effective size of facilities after internal subdivision

Agency	No. of Facilities Subdivided	Mean Effective Size	s.d.
Local Authority	31	9.4	6.9
Health Authority	9	6.3	4.2
Private Sector	2	11.4	5.0
Voluntary Sector	0	9.5	5.5
All facilities	42	8.9	6.1

Function

Aims

The prime objective of the study was to examine the cost and quality of residential services, but the facilities sampled served a wide range of functions in addition to the provision of long-term residential accommodation. As Table 2.4 shows, in 56 facilities the aim, as described by the officer in charge, was to provide a home for residents permanently or for as long as the resident wished. A further 41 had this as an aim for some residents, but also provided respite care or acted as a halfway house. In 18 facilities, the declared aim was to provide a halfway house but in very few of these was there a structured programme of rehabilitation requiring the person with learning disabilities to move on to another facility after a set period of time. Promoting independence was a prime aim of these facilities, but it was difficult to distinguish the service provided by many so-called 'halfway' houses from the developmental and rehabilitative activities taking place in homes providing more permanent accommodation.

Table 2.4 Declared aims of facilities

	Permanent Home	Halfway House	Mixed Functions	Other
Local Authority	10	9	21	16
Health Authority	24	4	9	3
Private Sector	15	2	5	2
Voluntary Sector	17	0	6	4
All	66	15	41	25

Respite services

Respite services were provided in 62 facilities (42 per cent) most notably amongst the Local Authorities (see Table 2.5). In most, this amounted to only one or two places but in seven (18 per cent) Local Authority, eight (50 percent) Health Authority and four (57 per cent) voluntary facilities, the proportion of respite beds comprised at least 20 per cent of the total number of available places.

Table 2.5 Number of facilities providing respite services

	Providing Any Respite Care	Respite Beds > 20% of Total Places
Local Authority	38	7
Health Authority	16	8
Private Sector	1	0
Voluntary Sector	7	4
All	62	19

Officers in charge were not asked explicitly about the pros and cons of providing respite care in the same premises as longer-term residential service, and none volunteered any information on the benefits of the arrangements. A number did comment, some quite vociferously, on the disadvantages, particularly of the disrupting effect of recurrent admissions on established residents and the disproportionate amount of staff time which short-stay clients needed and which led to the relative neglect of others. This was particularly so in two adult facilities which provided a respite service for children. In another small NHS facility, striving to provide a service based on the principles of normalization, the one respite bed was tolerated only because a proportion of the short-stay clients had established friendships with some of the residents.

Other services

Table 2.6 shows the number of facilities which provide additional services for people who are non-resident. Formal services tend to be day care provided on-site though, in one or two instances, it includes the provision of office space within the residential facility for members of community mental handicap teams or field social workers. One Health Authority facility acted as a resource centre for the local community, providing in addition to the six continuing care beds, 18 short-stay beds, offices for the community nursing service and clinical space for the psychiatrist, psychologist and other therapists.

Table 2.6 Facilities providing services for people who are non-resident

Agency	Formal Services	Informal Services	No Other Services
Local Authority	23	11	24
Health Authority	7	1	32
Private Sector	4	4	15
Voluntary sector	2	8	15
All	36	24	86

Informal services cover those which have evolved over time or which have been encouraged by the staff of the facility without the explicit or formal agreement of the management agency. These include recreational activities in the evenings and, in two instances, a 'drop-in' respite service. In the main, such services were being provided from within the resources in the facility.

Not all additional services provided in the residential facilities were aimed at people with a mental handicap. In one Local Authority unit, the kitchens were used to provide the meals for the Authority's meals on wheels service. In another facility, the day-room was used to provide day services for elderly people, while in the third, the day-room was used by the transport staff as a restroom. To facilitate this, they were required to bring in their own telephone and kettle!

The provision of additional services within residential facilities is an attempt to make the best use of scarce staffing and capital resources. However, such arrangements are hardly consistent with the principles of 'ordinary living' and it is questionable whether there are any direct benefits to the residents. The use of space in residential facilities for people who are not resident says much about the status as tenants of those clients for whom the facility is home. The resource centre, for example, had a relatively small lounge which, at the time of our visit, resembled a busy waiting-room rather than a sitting room.

Chapter 3

Intersectoral Comparisons of Environmental Quality

Summary

- Homeliness

  - Less than one-third of Local Authority homes were in ordinary houses compared to over 70 per cent of those provided by Health Authorities.

  - Local Authority and voluntary homes were significantly more likely to be closer to services for disabled people than homes run by the other sectors.

  - In two-thirds of all homes, the evening meal was served by 5.30 pm.

  - In one-third of homes, staff do not share a meal with the residents. Staff in the private sector were less likely to eat with the clients than staff in other sectors.

- Individualization

  - The time at which clients go to bed was flexible in 21 per cent of homes. In most there was a wide range of times at which residents go to bed.

  - Voluntary and private sector homes were more attractive and provided more individualized accommodation than the public sector homes.

  - Staff in private sector homes were more likely to talk to clients at mealtimes than staff in Local Authority homes.

  - Private sector homes were significantly less individually orientated in the management of day-to-day care of clients than homes in other sectors.

  - Clients in private homes were given less opportunity than clients in other sector homes to participate in activities relating to daily domestic life.

- Opportunities for clients to make decisions about their own daily lives were infrequent in all homes, but the Local Authority and voluntary homes provided most opportunities for them to do this and the private sector least.
- Almost all clients (98 per cent) had sole and continuous use of personal clothing and their own toiletries.
- The proportion of homes with key workers for clients was highest in Local Authorities and lowest in the private sector.
- Only 54 per cent of homes had Individual Programme Plans (IPPs) for clients. The proportion of clients with IPPs was highest in homes run by Health Authorities and lowest in homes run by Local Authorities.
- Local Authorities had the lowest number of clients with written plans specified for their needs.
- Clients in Local Authority homes were out more often during the week than clients in any other sector homes.
- More clients in voluntary homes went out at weekends than in any other sector.
- Significantly more clients in voluntary homes than any other sector used money or received training to do this.
- Shops and pubs were very close to most homes in all sectors but the majority of private sector homes are some distance from a Social Education Centre.
- Family contact was highest in voluntary sector homes and lowest in private sector homes.
- There was uniformly low contact with friends living in the community by clients in all sector homes.
- The majority of clients went on holiday with people from the homes in which they live and not with members of their family. There was no difference between the agencies.
- The use of community amenities was uniformly low in all sectors.

Introduction

Government policy documents have reiterated the importance of aspects of environmental quality in their own right, in the provision of residential facilities as part of community-based care. There is a recurring emphasis on small-scale homely environments. The service provided within these homely environments is to be one which reflects individual need, providing opportunities for growth and development and fostering links with the local community, encouraging the use of community resources available in addition to specialist services.

In this study, attempts were made to identify, both by describing and, where possible, measuring more systematically, the extent to which community-based residential facilities were characterized by:

- homeliness
- individualization of services providing opportunity for individual growth and development
- the use of locally available amenities and contact with family and friends.

The scale of the study permitted the psychometric testing of some existing measures; it also permitted the development of new measures. The whole approach to the measurement of environment in this study reflects the view that environments must be characterized as a series of dimensions (Pugh *et al.*, 1969). The interrelationship between these dimensions is a matter for empirical exploration. Similarly, it is assumed that the effect of environmental press on client performance and on cost is a matter of empirical enquiry.

The Environmental Quality Indicators

In the study, seven scales of environmental quality reported in the literature were used and four new ones developed in areas where no instruments were available. The seven established indicators are:

> The Physical Quality Index (Temple University, 1985 – see Raynes, 1988)
> The Room Rating Index (Temple University, 1985 – see Raynes, 1988)
> The Group Home Management Scale (revised) (Conroy and Bradley, 1985)
> The Index of Participation in Daily Living (Raynes and Sumpton, 1986)
> The Index of Adult Autonomy (Raynes and Sumpton, 1986)
> The Choice-making Scale (Conroy and Feinstein, 1986)
> The Index of Community Involvement (Raynes and Sumpton, 1986)

The four new ones are:

Mealtime Scale
Scale of Family Contact
Care Plans for Clients Scale
Scale of Contact with Friends

These provide a battery of instruments sensitive to environmental differences across agencies, as well as within them, and applicable in settings for adults with moderate or severe learning disabilities.

The presentation of the results, both the descriptive data and those resulting from the application of scales, is organized round the three major environmental areas identified as integral to community care in government policy documents. Twenty-eight aspects of the environments provided in the homes we visited were explored; ten relate to homeliness, 13 to individualized care and five to the use of locally available amenities and contact with family and friends.

Homeliness

Types of housing

One indicator of homeliness is the type of house in which services are provided. There are distinct inter-agency differences in the types of building used to house residential facilities (see Table 3.1). Local Authority Social Service Departments rely predominantly on functional purpose-built facilities (ie, hostels) though use is made of ordinary domestic property. Health Authorities are relatively unfettered by the legacy of past investment in purpose-built units and have been able to make greater use of housing stock of various sizes. Where facilities have been constructed, they tend to be campus-style designs with three or four separate small units (six to eight beds) grouped on the same site. Eleven facilities were located in two or more ordinary houses adjoining one another. In some, doorways had been made through dividing walls to provide a single unit. In others, the residents in each house lived separately and staff used front and rear doors to gain access to each part of the facility.

Independent sector facilities tend to be in larger houses, often boarding houses or country houses in their own grounds or in converted accommodation such as an old public house, an old nurses' home and several former vicarages.

Table 3.1 Type of building in which the facilities are located

Type of Building	Management Agency				
	LA	HA	Pte	Vol	TOTAL
HOUSING STOCK					
Small (1-4 places)	10	17	0	6	33
Medium (5-8 places)	2	10	7	8	27
Large (9+ places)	4	3	16	10	33
Adjoining Houses	6	3	1	1	11
FUNCTIONAL PROPERTY					
Small Units	2	0	0	1	3
Large Units	35	3	0	0	38
Campus-style	0	5	0	0	5
TOTAL	59	41	24	26	150

Location

Over one-half of the houses we visited were in suburban streets (51 per cent), 13 per cent were in urban streets (town centres) and 15 per cent in rural villages. Only 2 per cent were in isolated rural locations. Eighteen per cent of the houses were not classified.

Perhaps a better indicator of homeliness than location is the proximity of the ordinary house to other ordinary houses. One question on how close the house was to other homes or services for people with a disability was used to ascertain this information. Responses were rated thus:

1 = Glaring proximity of services for disabled people – can be seen from unit or is part of it, eg, would include hospital, elderly persons' home

2 = Moderate proximity – other services for disabled people nearby, eg, down the road, in the next street

3 = No other services for disabled people close by

4 = Valued juxtaposition/concentration.

We can see from Table 3.2 the proportion of facilities in each agency in categories 1 to 4.

Table 3.2 Location of homes in relation to other services for people with a disability (%)

Agency	Glaring	Moderate	None	Valued	No. of Cases
Local Authority	40	25	35	–	48
Health Authority	26	19	55	–	31
Private Sector	11	21	68	–	19
Voluntary Sector	38	25	31	–	16
Total Percentage	31	23	46	–	114

A sample index of proximity to other specialist services was constructed summing the scores on this item. This gave an overall mean score of 2.13. Table 3.3 shows the agency scores on this index of normalization.

Table 3.3 Index of proximity to other services for people with a disability

	Mean Score	s.d.	No. of Cases
Local Authority	1.96	0.87	48
Health Authority	2.29	0.86	31
Private Sector	2.58	0.69	19
Voluntary Sector	1.80	0.98	16
Overall	2.13	0.89	114

An analysis of variance showed that the difference between agency types in this aspect of ordinariness or homeliness of the facility was statistically significantly (F=3.45, d.f.=3,122 p<0.01). The voluntary agency homes and those run by Local Authorities were significantly more likely to be located near services for other disabled people than were homes run by the Health Authorities and the private sector.

Times of daily events

The daily rhythm of life, as represented by the time of meals, getting up and going to bed, may also give some indication of homeliness.

In 95 facilities (64 per cent), residents could get up when they wanted, though in 69 of these the residents apparently chose to get up at the same time as each other every morning. In over half of the residences (55 per cent), the clients began to get up between 7 and 7.30. The remainder began to get up at a later time, except in eight facilities (5 per cent) where residents were getting up during the week at 6.30 or earlier. In five of these, the early start was determined by the resident's working commitments, but in three facilities there was no such reason.

Evening mealtimes still seem to be early and inflexible for the majority of residents, as Table 3.4 shows. In 39 per cent of residences, it was claimed that the evening meal was served at a time determined by the residents or by staffs' understanding of their needs. However, flexibility in the time the meal is actually served was only evident in 14 per cent of homes, and in 66 per cent of the residences the evening meal was served by 5.30.

Table 3.4 Mealtimes

Time Evening Meal Served	No.	%
4.30 or earlier	12	8
5.00 or 5.30	87	58
6.00 or 6.30	27	18
7.00 or later	2	1
Flexible times	21	14

At this and other mealtimes in the majority of the homes (64 per cent), it was usual for staff to eat with residents. It was not the practice at all in 12 per cent of the homes. In a further 22 per cent of the facilities visited, staff either ate sitting at a separate table or didn't eat but sat with the residents. Thus in over one-third of the homes, staff did not share a meal with clients on a day-to-day basis. This is perhaps one of the best indicators of homeliness. Staff in private sector homes were less likely to eat with the residents than staff in other settings (see Table 3.5).

Table 3.5 Percentage of homes in which staff eat with clients

Agency	Eat with Clients	Eat at Special Table or Sit but Don't Eat	Don't Eat with Clients	No Information
Local Authority	60	28	10	2
Health Authority	68	20	12	–
Private Sector	50	25	25	–
Voluntary Sector	77	12	4	8
Overall	64	22	12	2

The earliest time at which residents began to go to bed was 6.00 pm in one home. However, according to staff, this time was determined by their perceptions of the needs of the residents. The time the residents went to bed was described as completely flexible or determined by the residents' needs in 117 (80 per cent) of the facilities. Yet most residents apparently chose to go to bed at the same time each night and actual bedtimes were only variable in 30 facilities (21 per cent). In most homes, there was a wide range of time between the first and last residents going to bed, but in 13 homes there were fixed bedtimes for all residents. Some of these were in homes which had no night-staff and where it was policy for day-staff to ensure residents were in bed with windows and doors locked, electric plugs removed, etc. before they finished duty. In one home (which did have night-staff) the set bed time was 7.00 pm.

Physical environment

We used two measures of this: the Physical Quality Instrument and a Room Rating measure.

The Physical Quality Instrument

Details of the scale developed by Temple University (1985, see Raynes, 1988) were given in Chapter 1. The scores range from 0 to 18 on this measure, the higher score representing pleasant and attractive facilities in which high levels of individuality and variation were shown. Data were available for 115 cases, being missing on some items for 34 (23 per cent) of the 150 homes. The overall mean score on this scale is 12.06, with a standard deviation of 3.35 for the 115 cases. Table 3.6 shows the mean scale scores on this measure for each of the agency types.

Table 3.6 Scores on the Physical Quality Instrument

Agency	Mean PQI Score	s.d.	No. of Cases
Local Authority	10.35	3.12	43
Health Authority	11.89	2.88	35
Private Sector	14.24	2.88	21
Voluntary Sector	14.19	2.86	16
Overall	12.06	3.35	115

An analysis of variance indicated a significant difference between groups (F=11.29, d.f.=3,115, p<0.001). The private and voluntary sector scores on this measure were significantly higher than those of the public sector homes. These homes were clearly more attractive and more individualized than those provided by Local or Health Authorities.

Room Ratings

The measure of the homeliness in each room of the homes was carried out using an instrument developed by Temple University (1985, see Raynes, 1988). The Room Rating scale covers five aspects of the room: its general appearance, the condition of the furniture in it, its lightness, its freshness, and its resemblance to 'ordinary' family rooms; details were given in Chapter 1. The higher score reflects an environment which is neat and well maintained, airy and fresh smelling. Scores on each of these room ratings is from 0 to 15 and are given in Table 3.7. An analysis of variance was carried out but there are no significant differences between the sectors. The scores reflect rooms which, on average, are clean, appeared lived in, with furniture in sound condition, and are adequately ventilated with no unpleasant odours.

Table 3.7 Scores on Room Rating Scale

Agency	Room Rating Scale							
	Bedroom		Living Room		Kitchen		Bathroom	
	Mean	s.d.	Mean	s.d.	Mean	s.d.	Mean	s.d.
Local Authority	9.3	2.2	10.1	1.5	10.2	1.4	10.1	1.7
Health Authority	10.5	1.9	10.6	1.8	10.7	1.4	10.5	1.7
Private Sector	11.2	1.9	11.2	1.7	10.9	1.6	11.3	2.0
Voluntary Sector	10.3	2.5	10.3	2.0	10.1	1.2	10.5	2.0
Overall	10.1	2.2	10.5	1.7	10.4	1.4	10.5	1.9

Mealtimes

We were able to observe a mealtime in some of the homes we visited. A record was made of the way tables were set, whether staff and clients spoke to each other during the meal and whether clients had to sit and wait for any length of time before and after meals. Data for the four items were available in only 43 homes. Scale scores range from 0 to 8, the higher score reflecting the more homely environment. The mean scores on this measure are given in Table 3.8. The measure did not differentiate between homes run by different agencies.

Table 3.8 Mealtime Scale scores

Agency	Mean Score	s.d.	No. of Cases
Local Authority	6.68	1.29	19
Health Authority	6.92	1.21	14
Private Sector	7.67	0.82	6
Voluntary Sector	5.50	2.89	4
Overall	6.79	1.46	43

Staff talked to clients during meals in all agency settings but this occurred most frequently in private sector homes (86 per cent), and least frequently in Local Authority homes, (46 per cent of those observed). There was no conversation at all in 23 per cent of Local

Authority homes, 16 per cent of Health Authority homes and 29 per cent of voluntary homes.

Individualization of Services Providing Opportunities for Growth and Development

In this section we report data on 13 aspects of individualization of care and the provision of opportunities for individual growth and development. These are:

1. Management of aspects of daily life
2. Participation in domestic life
3. Adult autonomy
4. Client choice making
5. Clients' clothing
6. Clients' personal possessions
7. Use of key workers
8. Use of individual programme plans
9. Use of written plans for clients
10. Use of daytime activities
11. Clients' evening activities
12. Clients' weekend activities
13. Training in the use of money.

Items 1 to 4 were measured using established scales. A new scale was developed from the data for item 10. Single questions were asked about all of the other aspects.

Management of aspects of daily life

This was explored using the revised Group Homes Management Scale (Conroy and Bradley, 1985) which was described in Chapter 1. It measures the extent to which different practices are resident-oriented, flexible and individually based or reflect staff control and institutional needs. Data were not available for all of the items on all 149 facilities, so 19 were excluded from the scaling. Table 3.9 shows the scores by agency. Scores range from 0 to 30; high scores reflect resident-oriented care.

Table 3.9 Mean scores on the Group Home Management Scale

Agency	Mean GHMS Score	s.d.	No. of Cases
Local Authority	18.1	7.6	55
Health Authority	17.7	6.1	36
Private Sector	12.6	7.6	19
Voluntary Sector	18.3	6.1	20
Overall	17.2	7.2	130

None of the residences scored particularly highly on this measure and it is clear that the private facilities were more institutionally-oriented than the facilities run by the other three agencies. An analysis of variance showed the difference between the groups to be significant (F=3.23, d.f.=3,127, p<0.02).

Participation in domestic life

This was explored using the Index of Participation in Domestic Life described in Chapter 1 (Raynes and Sumpton, 1986). Lower scores on this measure reflect greater opportunities for involvement in activities of daily living, eg, food preparation. Scores range from 13 to 39. Table 3.10 shows the scores on the scale by agency.

Table 3.10 Index of Participation in Domestic Life scores

	Mean	s.d.	No. of Cases
Local Authority	28.4	7.3	699
Health Authority	29.7	7.8	211
Private Sector	31.9	6.1	203
Voluntary Sector	26.4	6.7	167
Overall	28.9	7.3	1280

A one-way ANOVA shows a significant difference among agencies (F=20.6, d.f.-3,1276, p<0.001). Subsequent Scheffe tests indicate significant differences between the Local Authority and voluntary sector, between the Health Authority and voluntary sector and between the Private sector and the other three agencies (<0.05).

Private sector homes' scores were higher, indicating less opportunity to participate in activities of daily living.

Adult autonomy

This was explored using the Index of Adult Autonomy (IAA) which measures the extent to which clients have control over aspects of their daily life. The higher the score the more control the individual has over various activities. The scale is described in Chapter 1. Table 3.11 shows the mean scale scores, standard deviation and number of cases within agency on the IAA.

Table 3.11 Index of Adult Autonomy scores

	Mean	s.d.	No. of Cases
Local Authority	13.6	4.2	635
Health Authority	10.6	5.1	187
Private Sector	11.7	4.0	190
Voluntary Sector	13.6	4.3	155
Overall	12.8	4.5	1167

A one-way ANOVA shows a significant difference among agencies (F=28.6, d.f.=3,1163, p<0.001). Scheffe tests show significant differences between the Local and Health Authorities, between the Local Authority and private sector, between the voluntary and private sectors, and between the voluntary sector and the Health Authority.

The Local Authority and voluntary agency homes provide more opportunity for individual control over activities than do either the Health Authority or private homes. Least opportunity for control by the clients is provided in Health Authority homes.

Choice making

This was explored using the Choice-making Scale which was developed by Conroy and Feinstein (1986) and consists of 24 items to cover opportunities for making choices in the area of food, own house or room, clothes, sleeping, waking and recreation. The scale was described in Chapter 1. Scale scores range from 24 to 96; the higher the score the more opportunity the client is given for making choices. The mean scale standard deviation and number of cases for which these are available are given in Table 3.12.

Table 3.12 Choice-making Scale scores

	Mean	s.d.	No. of Cases
Local Authority	73.0	16.1	578
Health Authority	62.2	23.6	178
Private Sector	65.4	17.5	143
Voluntary Sector	73.9	15.5	147
Overall	70.2	18.2	1046

A one-way ANOVA shows a significant difference among agencies, (F=22.4, d.f. 3,1042, p< .001). Subsequent Scheffe tests indicate significant differences between Local Authority and Health Authority scale scores, between Local Authority and private agencies, between voluntary agencies and Health Authority and between the voluntary and private sectors.

Homes run by Local Authorities or by the voluntary sector provided more opportunities for choice than homes in Health Authorities or in the private sector.

Clothing and personal possessions

We ascertained if the clients all had exclusive use of nine items of clothing, following King *et al.* (1971), and if clients had their own toiletries, jewellery, radio or cassette player and television.

The lowest percentage of clients possessing each of the items of clothing was 98 per cent. In the case of personal possessions, 98 per cent of all clients had their own toiletries, 73 per cent had jewellery and 84 per cent of all clients had either a radio, cassette or a television of their own. There was no difference between the agencies in terms of the proportion of clients who had either the clothing specified or the personal possessions.

Key workers and IPPs

One managerial development to try to ensure personalized care and support for a client in residential settings has been the designation of a staff member as a 'key worker'. One individual staff member takes responsibility for coordinating, planning and implementing specific aspects of planned services to a client. The concept has been implemented to varying degrees as Table 3.13 indicates.

Table 3.13 Percentage of clients with a key worker

	Yes	No	No. of Cases
Local Authority	91	9	728
Health Authority	79	21	234
Private Sector	63	37	215
Voluntary Sector	65	35	170
Overall	81	19	1347

Clearly, in Local Authority homes this strategy had been almost universally implemented. A high percentage of clients in Health Authority homes also had key workers but over a third of clients in the private and voluntary sectors did not. The difference between the private and voluntary sectors and other homes is statistically significant (chi-square = 126.5, d.f.=3, p<0.001).

Another tool for ensuring individual care and support for the client is the Individualised Programme Plan, (NDG, 1980). We can see from Table 3.14 that only just over half of all clients have IPPs, despite the high proportion who had key workers.

Table 3.14 Percentage of clients with IPPs

	Yes	No	No. of Cases
Local Authority	45	55	709
Health Authority	72	28	229
Private Sector	53	47	208
Voluntary Sector	67	33	166
Overall	54	46	1312

It is in the Health Authority homes that this method of planning and supporting individuals is used most (chi-square=62.8, d.f.=3, p<0.001). In those homes where IPPs were used, the majority were reviewed on a six-monthly basis. However, as Table 3.15 shows, in Local Authority and voluntary sector homes there were fewer clients being reviewed this frequently than in the other sector homes.

Table 3.15 Frequency (%) of IPP reviews

	Six-monthly	Yearly	No. of Cases
Local Authority	64	36	339
Health Authority	89	11	170
Private Sector	89	11	110
Voluntary Sector	67	32	109
Overall	74	26	728

Written plans for clients

To ensure individualized support, client needs have to be identified. Thus, we asked whether written plans were available for clients in eight defined areas of need.

Plans were most frequently found relating to the clients' residential care needs, recreational needs, community-skill needs and their medical and emotional needs, but the proportion of clients for whom such planning was done was not very high, as Table 3.16 shows.

Table 3.16 Percentage of clients with written plans relating to their needs

	Yes	No
Employment needs	21	66
Medical needs	50	40
Family contact needs	42	47
Residential care needs	66	26
Emotional needs	50	37
Self-help skills	45	45
Community skills	51	39
Recreational activities	53	37

We used these data to create a simple additive scale with eight items and scores ranging from 8 to 16. The lower the score, the more likely there are to be written plans in various areas. The mean and standard deviation scores on this score by agency are given in Table 3.17.

Table 3.17 Scores on Care Plan for Clients scale

	Mean	s.d.	No. of Cases
Local Authority	12.3	2.6	552
Health Authority	11.5	2.9	155
Private Sector	11.9	2.4	165
Voluntary Sector	11.9	2.7	139
Overall	12.1	2.7	1011

There is a significant difference among the agencies (F=3.6, df=3, 1007, p<0.05). Scheffe tests indicate a significant difference between the Local Authority and Health Authority homes. Written plans were found less frequently in Local Authority homes than in homes of the other three agencies.

Daytime activities

Part of meeting clients needs involves finding activities for them to be involved in during the day, some of which will take them out of their homes. We found that 62 per cent of the clients went out every weekday and only 3 per cent (42 people) did not go out at all during the week. Table 3.18 shows the average number of days clients went out during the week by agency type.

Table 3.18 The mean number of days that clients go out

	Mean	s.d.	No. of Cases
Local Authority	4.7	0.9	670
Health Authority	4.2	1.4	200
Private Sector	4.2	1.3	203
Voluntary Sector	4.5	1.1	148
Overall	4.5	1.1	1221

A one-way ANOVA shows a significant difference among agencies (F = 16.6, df 3,1217, p<.001). Scheffe tests indicate a significant difference between the Local Authority and private sector, and between the Local Authority and Health Authority. Clients living in Local Authority homes were out more often during the week than clients in any other kind of home, though the difference (significant in a statistical sense) amounts to no more than a half day per week.

The kinds of activities in which clients are involved during the week involve them mainly with other people with learning disabilities. The most common location for their activities is a training or social education centre or hospital day centre. Almost a quarter of residents received no formal day services other than those provided by staff in the residential facility (see Table 3.19).

Table 3.19 Main daily activity

Agency	Percentage of Residents			
	Day Centre	Employment	Education	No Formal Service
Local Authority	80.6	4.3	3.2	11.8
Health Authority	54.1	5.9	8.6	31.4
Private Sector	46.4	3.8	2.8	46.9
Voluntary Sector	65.0	11.1	–	25.0
All Residents	68.5	5.4	3.6	22.5

Evening and weekend activities

In addition to daytime activities, clients' needs for recreation both in the evenings and at weekends have to be addressed. We explored the extent to which these needs were met by asking:

1. How many evenings during the week the client went out.

2. What kinds of activities in the evening the client was involved in, and whether they were specifically for people with learning disabilities.

3. The number of days at the weekend the client went out of the house.

One quarter of clients did not go out at all on weekday evenings. Table 3.20 shows the mean number of evenings clients went out, by agency type.

Table 3.20 The mean number of evenings that clients go out during the week, within agency

	Mean	s.d.	No. of Cases
Local Authority	3.2	1.9	646
Health Authority	3.4	2.0	193
Private Sector	3.1	2.9	199
Voluntary Sector	3.3	2.0	150
Overall	3.2	2.0	1188

Relatively small numbers of clients in each agency went to activities during the week which were exclusively for people with learning disabilities. Of those going out, only 16 per cent in Local Authorities, 11 per cent in Health Authorities, 8 per cent in private homes and 18 per cent in voluntary homes went out to events organized solely for people with learning disabilities.

Going out and about at the weekend was common. In all settings, 76 per cent of all clients had been out either on one or both days at the weekend. Table 3.21 shows the proportion of clients from each type of home going out on one or both days at the weekend.

Table 3.21 Percentage of clients who went out over the previous weekend, within agency

	Out One Day	Out Both Days	Not Out	No. of Cases
Local Authority	42	33	25	735
Health Authority	39	32	29	229
Private Sector	43	36	21	216
Voluntary Sector	37	46	17	166
Overall	41	35	24	1346

A chi-square test shows a significant difference among agencies (chi-square=14.6, df=6, $p<0.05$). Significantly more clients living in voluntary homes were out at weekends than clients in other types of homes.

Training to use money

Living in the community requires some skill in the handling of money if the independence of the client is to be promoted. We asked whether clients were involved in training programmes to assist them in this area. Twenty nine per cent of clients were said to be able to use money with little assistance, 35 per cent were receiving training and 35 per cent were said to be not capable of benefiting from any training. There are significant differences between the homes run by the different types of agency in terms of the proportion of clients within them fitting into these categories, as Table 3.22 shows.

Table 3.22 The percentage of clients who receive training in money handling, within agency

Agency	No – Not Capable	No – Can Use With Little Assistance	Yes	No. of Cases
Local Authority	31	34	35	689
Health Authority	49	23	28	224
Private Sector	39	23	38	208
Voluntary Sector	30	27	43	166
Overall	35	29	35	1287

A chi-square test shows a significant difference among agencies (chi-square=34.1, df=6, $p<0.001$).

Use of Locally Available Amenities and Contact with Family and Friends

In this section we report data on five aspects of the use of locally available amenities and contact with family and friends. These are:

1. Proximity of amenities
2. Contact with family members
3. Contact with friends
4. Holidays
5. Frequency of use of community amenities.

Items 1 and 3 were covered by single questions. Items 2 and 4 used scales developed in this study, and item 5 used an established scale.

Proximity of amenities

Whether or not one becomes part of a neighbourhood and uses local amenities is affected by a number of factors. One of these, which is reasonably easily identified, is the distance of the home in which you live from specified local amenities. We asked staff to tell us whether each of seven amenities were accessible on foot (ie, within a 20-minute walk) or needed transport to get to them. If transport were necessary, we asked whether the transport available was public transport or some other form such as staff cars or transport specifically assigned for the use of the home. The amenities we asked about were shops, post offices, pubs, leisure facilities, education or training centre (SEC), dentists and doctors. The responses are given in Table 3.23. Most homes are within walking distance of a leisure centre and over 60 per cent of them are within walking distance of a doctor and a dentist. There is little difference between the homes with regard to access to these amenities.

Table 3.23 Percentage of homes within 20-minutes walk of local amenities

Agency	Shop	PO	Pub	Leisure	SEC	Dentist	GP
Local Authority	98	91	95	56	45	69	62
Health Authority	100	95	100	49	24	71	58
Private Sector	88	96	96	67	13	54	71
Voluntary Sector	96	96	92	54	27	58	58
Overall	97	94	96	55	31	65	62

Staff in the homes differed in the extent to which they were satisfied with the transport available to get to local amenities. Fifty-eight per cent of Local Authority staff were either satisfied or very satisfied, compared with 78 per cent of Health Authority staff, 73 per cent voluntary homes staff and 100 per cent of private homes staff.

Family

Part of the network of support in the community for clients will hopefully be family and friends. We asked about the extent to which there was contact by clients with their families and friends. Visits by family to the clients homes were not very frequent for most clients in all types of homes. Nineteen per cent of all clients were visited weekly by their families, 22 per cent had contact other than a visit with their families on a weekly basis and 16 per cent of clients went home on a weekly basis to their families. Twenty-one per cent of all clients had no contact with their family in the form of a visit to them, 29 per cent had no other contact with their family, and 42 per cent of clients never went to their family's home.

A Scale of Family Contact was derived from the items relating to contact with clients' families. The scores range from 3 to 12; the lower the score the greater the possible family contact. Seven per cent of clients had scores of 3 on this scale indicating weekly contact with families and 90 per cent had scores of 12 indicating the lowest levels of contact. Table 3.24 shows the mean Family Contact Scale score and standard deviation within agency.

Table 3.24 Family Contact Scale scores

	Mean	s.d.	No. of Cases
Local Authority	8.0	2.6	679
Health Authority	8.2	2.7	208
Private Sector	8.5	2.5	190
Voluntary Sector	7.5	2.4	144
Overall	8.0	2.6	1221

A one-way analysis of variance shows that the difference among agencies is significant (F=4.8, df=3,1217 p<0.01). Scheffe tests show a significant difference between the private and voluntary homes (p<0.05).

Friends

The responses to our questions concerning contact with friends indicated that this is very small indeed. Only 10 per cent of clients had been visited by a friend on a weekly basis and only 14 per cent went to friends as often as this. A Scale of Contact with Friends was derived from these data. The score ranges from 2 to 8 with the lower score indicating the greater contact with friends. Six per cent of clients obtained the lower score, indicating weekly contact with friends, and 17 per cent the highest score, indicating no contact with friends. The mean score on this measure for each type of home is given in Table 3.25.

Table 3.25 Score on Scale of Contact with Friends

	Mean	s.d.	No. of Cases
Local Authority	5.8	1.9	529
Health Authority	5.9	2.0	156
Private Sector	5.8	1.8	154
Voluntary Sector	5.6	1.6	146
Overall	5.8	1.8	985

There is no difference between the agencies in terms of the scores on this measure. Across all settings, the majority of clients had little contact with friends in their neighbourhood.

Holidays

The majority of clients (80 per cent) did not go away on a holiday with their families in the year preceding our visit to their home. However, 82 per cent of clients had been on a holiday with other clients in their residence. There was no difference between agencies in the uniformly high percentage of clients getting away for a holiday organized by the home in which they live, in the year preceding our visit. This is clear in Table 3.26, which shows the proportion of clients going on such a holiday.

Table 3.26 Percentage of clients who went on a holiday organized by the residence or family last year

	Yes	No	No. of Cases
Local Authority	82	18	738
Health Authority	83	17	234
Private Sector	79	21	215
Voluntary Sector	87	13	173
Overall	82	18	1360

Frequency of use of community amenities

This was measured using the Index of Community Involvement (ICI) (Raynes and Sumpton, 1986) which consists of 15 items, 14 of which ascertain whether clients have used specified facilities in the community within the past four weeks. The fifteenth item relates to participating in a holiday within the previous 12 months (see Chapter 1 for details of this instrument).

The possible range of scores on this item is from 0 to 60. The higher score represents maximum involvement in the community. Data were available on all 15 items for facilities; the mean score for these facilities was 26.2. This suggests that the degree of involvement in community activities in all types of home was not very great. The mean scores on the ICI are given in Table 3.27.

Table 3.27 Index of Community Involvement scores

	Mean ICI Score	s.d.	No. of Cases
Local Authority	24.93	9.8	55
Health Authority	25.22	8.5	40
Private Sector	27.22	9.2	23
Voluntary Sector	29.56	7.7	25
Overall	26.19	9.1	143

An analysis of variance showed that the difference between the mean scores of the four agency types on this measure was not significant.

The Battery of Environmental Measures

Twenty-eight aspects of the environments provided in the homes we visited were explored. Seventeen of these were accessed by the use of single questions providing us with descriptive information. Single questions concerned:

1. The type of property
2. The location of the home
3. Proximity of home to other ordinary homes
4. What time clients got up
5. Evening mealtimes
6. Staff eating with clients

7. What time clients went to bed
8. Clients' clothing
9. Clients' personal possessions
10. Whether clients had a key worker
11. Whether there were IPPs for clients
12. Type of daily activity the clients were involved in and how often
13. How often clients went out during the weekday evenings
14. How often clients went out at weekends
15. Training of clients to use money
16. Whether local amenities accessible on foot
17. Client's holidays.

The remaining areas listed below were rated by using scales:

1. Homeliness
2. Individualized care: fostering growth and development
3. Local amenities and contact with family and friends.

Not all of the measures discriminated between homes of different agency types (see Figure 3.1). The ICI and the Contact with Friends Scale both indicated that there was uniformly low use of local amenities and infrequent contact with friends. Similarly, the room rating scale did not distinguish between the agencies.

Further analysis of these measures could ascertain what degree of overlap there is between them and the extent to which they are uniquely tapping the factors identified as homeliness, individualized care and the use of local services and contact with family and friends.

Figure 3.1 Scales of environmental quality

Measure (No. of Items)	Means of Obtaining Data and Direction of Scoring	Internal Reliability Level (Standardized Alpha Coefficient)	Statistic Used to Ascertain Discriminatory Power	Significance Level
HOMELINESS				
Physical Quality Instrument (6 Items)	Observation Higher scores = Most homely	.641	F = 11.29	***
Room Rating Measure (5 Items)	Observation Higher scores = Most homely			
Bathroom	Observation	.678	F = 2.7	*
Bedroom	Observation	.698	F = 4.6	**
Kitchen	Observation	.533	— — —	NS
Living Room	Observation Higher score = Most homely	.570	— — —	NS
Mealtimes (4 Items)	Observation Lower score = most homely	.669	F = 1.9	NS
INDIVIDUALIZED CARE				
Group Homes Management Scale (10 items)	Interview Higher Scores = Most individualized care	.843	F = 3.23	*

Measure (No. of Items)	Means of Obtaining Data and Direction of Scoring	Internal Reliability Level (Standardized Alpha Coefficient)	Statistic Used to Ascertain Discriminatory Power	Significance Level
Index of Participation in Domestic Life (3 Items)	Self-administered questionnaire for individuals Higher scores = most individualized care	.93	F = 20.6	***
Index of Adult Autonomy (11 Items)	ditto	.82	F = 28.6	***
Choice Making Scale (24 Items)	ditto	.96	F = 22.4	***
Care Plans for Clients (8 Items)	ditto	.84	F = 3.6	*
USE OF LOCAL SERVICES AND NETWORKS				
ICI (15 Items)	Interview Higher Scores = High use of local amenities	.70	- - -	NS
Family Contact Scale (3 Items)	Self-Administered questionnaire for individuals Lower scores = most contact with family	.74	F = 4.8	**
Friends Contact Scale (2 Items)	ditto	.70	- - -	NS

Key: * Significant at 90%   ** Significant at 95%   *** Significant at 99%

Chapter 4

Staffing

Summary

- Staff ratios were twice as high in Health Authority facilities as in those run by other agencies.
- The majority of first-line managers were trained in Local and Health Authority homes; this was not the case in the other sectors.
- Staff morale was lowest in the public sector homes.
- Staff morale was higher where communication between staff was satisfactory.
- Staff attitudes to people with learning disabilities were positive across all types of homes but more positive amongst first-line managers than direct care staff.
- The majority of all home visits by middle-line managers occurred less than once a week.
- The majority of middle managers had a specialist brief for services for people with learning disabilities.
- Private sector homes provided least staff training.
- Staff meetings occurred less than once a week in the majority of public sector homes.
- In the majority of homes first-line managers had control of the daily menu, the heating and other aspects of the day-to-day running of the homes.
- The delegation of fiscal control to facility managers was highest in the private and voluntary sectors. It was most limited in Local Authority facilities.
- Staff turnover was higher in NHS facilities than in Local Authorities. In the Local Authority sector, higher turnover was associated with smaller facilities.

Data Sources

Data about staff in the homes were obtained from three sources: the staff questionnaire, the interview with officers in charge, and the central services questionnaire.

Number of Staff

Mean staff ratios for each agency expressed as the number of whole-time equivalent staff members per resident are given in Table 4.1.

Table 4.1 Staffing ratios by agency

Agency	Mean	s.d.	No. of Homes
Local Authority	0.82	0.91	57
Health Authority	1.34	0.83	38
Private Sector	0.65	0.21	23
Voluntary Sector	0.85	0.50	25
Overall	0.94	0.79	143

The length of time staff in these homes had worked with people with learning disabilities is shown in Table 4.2.

Table 4.2 Length of time staff had worked with people with learning disabilities (%)

Agency	Less than 6 Months	6 Months to 2 Years	2 to 10 Years	More than 10 Years
Local Authority	3	17	52	27
Health Authority	5	18	54	23
Private Sector	11	26	43	19
Voluntary Sector	9	17	46	27
Overall	6	20	50	24

Almost a quarter of all staff had worked for more than ten years with people with learning disabilities and one half had been working between two and ten years. The Local Authority homes and those in the voluntary sector had more than a quarter of their staff with ten or more years of experience of working with people with learning disabilities. Both Local and Health Authority homes had more than half of their staff with at least two years experience in this field. A third of the staff in the non-statutory sector as compared with less than a quarter in the statutory agencies had staff with less than two years experience of working with people with learning disabilities.

Staff Turnover

The number of staff leaving each residential facility in the statutory sector was obtained from personnel officers and used to calculate a crude turnover rate. This was defined simply as the average number of people leaving the staffing establishment expressed as a percentage of the total establishment. A more sophisticated exercise, looking at turnover in whole-time equivalents or by grade of staff was not warranted given the prime objectives of the study. The ratio provides a crude measure of turnover but more importantly also reflects the numbers of relationships a resident must either make or break in the course of a year. The ratio therefore provides another indicator of quality of the service.

Table 4.3 Staff turnover in the statutory sector

Agency	% Staff Leaving	s.d.	No. of Cases
Local Authority	21.8	23.0	44
Health Authority	29.1	27.3	34
Statutory Sector	25.0	25.1	78

In the statutory sector as a whole, one quarter of staff left and were replaced each year, though turnover was higher in Health Authority facilities. Turnover was negatively related to the size of facilities, ie, larger facilities have lower staff turnover ($p<0.05$). However, this relationship held only for Local Authority facilities when each statutory agency was considered separately. In Health Authority homes, there was no clear relationship between staff turnover and size of facility.

Staff Training

First-line managers

A variety of titles, such as officer in charge, charge nurse, manager, were used by first-line managers in the different settings we visited. We chose the title of 'first-line managers' to designate people with responsibility for other care staff and charged with the day-to-day accountability and responsibility for running the homes. Not all first-line managers were trained. Overall, nearly a quarter were untrained. Table 4.4 shows the type of training, within each agency, of first-line managers.

Table 4.4 Type of training of first-line managers by agency (%)

Agency	Nursing	Social Work	Social Work and Nursing	Other Qualifications	No Qualifications	No Information
Local Authority	15	32	5	14	25	9
Health Authority	90	2	–	–	7	1
Private Sector	25	17	4	8	42	4
Voluntary Sector	32	9	–	24	28	5
Overall	40	17	3	11	23	5

Not surprisingly, the majority of first-line managers working for Health Authorities were nurse-trained. It is notable that only one-third of the first-line managers in Local Authority homes were trained in social work and 42 per cent of the first-line managers in the private sector had no training at all. The number of other staff who had either or both nursing or social work training was very small. Table 4.5 shows this clearly.

Table 4.5 Percentage of qualified other staff by agency

Agency	Mean Percentage Qualified	s.d.	No. of Cases
Local Authority	14.5	13.5	51
Health Authority	28.7	17.1	38
Private Sector	14.3	15.2	24
Voluntary Sector	12.5	15.8	25
Overall	18.0	16.5	138

Staff Morale and Staff Communication

A measure developed by Willcocks *et al.* (1987) was used to assess staff morale. This has 18 items, each of which is rated on a seven-point rating scale. Higher scores reflect higher levels of satisfaction with aspects of work. The range of scores is from 0 to 18. We have carried out psychometric testing of this measure and it has been shown to be a highly reliable instrument. (Details of this measure were given in Chapter 1.)

Two measures of satisfaction with communication were constructed (they were discussed in detail in Chapter 1). The first, communication with line managers, reflects staff satisfaction with opportunities to discuss aspects of their work with their first-line manager. The aspects of their work were:

1. The residents
2. The job to be done and ways to do it
3. Other work-related matters, for example hours of work or pay.

The second measure, communication with colleagues, explored how satisfied staff were with the opportunities they had to discuss the same aspects of their work with their immediate colleagues. The higher score on both measures reflects most satisfaction.

The measure of staff morale and the measures of satisfaction with communication have been described in a separate paper (Raynes *et al.*, 1990). The main findings, each of which was statistically significant at conventional levels, can be summarized thus:

1. The morale of staff in homes run by statutory agencies was lower than that of staff in either the private or voluntary sector homes.

2. The morale of domestic staff was lower than that of all other types of staff in homes across all agency types.

3. Staff morale was higher within homes in each type of agency where communication between staff and line managers and between colleagues was considered to be most satisfactory.

4. The morale of staff in all non-private homes was not affected by the level of satisfaction first-line managers expressed about their communication with their immediate managers, the middle managers in the system in which they operate.

Staff Attitudes to People with Learning Disabilities

We used a measure developed by Allen *et al.* (1985) to assess staff attitudes to people with a learning disability. This scale consists of eight items. Scale scores range from 8 to 40, with the higher score reflecting a positive and developmental approach to people with a mental handicap. The details of the measure and the findings relating to its application have been described in a separate paper (Raynes *et al.*, 1991). The main findings in this paper can be summarized as follows:

- Overall, staff attitudes were very positive. The score obtained by staff in the private homes was significantly lower than that for staff in the other agencies' homes.

- The attitudes of first-line managers were more positive in all agency types than the attitudes of direct care staff. These were more positive in all agency types than the attitudes of domestic staff.

- Staff attitudes to people with learning disabilities were more positive in smaller homes than in larger homes within each of the four agency settings.

Staff Organization

We asked line managers to indicate their level of satisfaction with the support they obtained from their line managers and to tell us how often they were visited by them. Table 4.6 shows the frequency of visits by middle managers to homes for each kind of agency. Data were available for 114 of the homes. None of the private facilities was asked this question because interviews took place with the owners of the facilities.

Table 4.6 Frequency of visits by middle managers to homes (%)

Agency	Daily	Weekly	Less Often
Local Authority	2	35	64
Health Authority	13	38	50
Voluntary Sector	–	42	58
Overall	5	37	58

In half or more of the homes, first-line managers were visited less often than weekly by their middle managers. However, the majority of first-line managers in Health and Local Authority homes were satisfied with the support they got from their middle managers. This was not the case in the voluntary sector. There, over one quarter expressed dissatisfaction with the kind of support they received from their middle managers. Table 4.7 summarizes the degree of satisfaction with middle managers expressed by first-line managers in the homes. The private sector was excluded from this part of the analysis.

Table 4.7 Satisfaction expressed by first-line managers in homes with middle managers (%)

Agency	Satisfactory	Neutral	Unsatisfactory
Local Authority	86	2	12
Health Authority	74	7	18
Voluntary Sector	58	16	26
Overall	77	6	17

We explored the extent to which middle managers were themselves specialists in the field of learning disabilities by asking the first-line managers for information about this. Table 4.8 summarizes our findings. Again, private sector homes were excluded.

Table 4.8 Middle managers as specialists in mental handicap (%)

Agency	Specialist	Generic
Local Authority	65	35
Health Authority	93	8
Voluntary Sector	58	42
Overall	73	26

The middle managers in the homes run by Health Authorities were almost all specialists in services for people with learning disabilities. This was true for almost two-thirds of those who were middle managers of Local Authority homes and 58 per cent of those in voluntary homes. Data were not available for 35 homes in this part of the analysis, 24 of which were private homes.

Staff Development

In the majority of homes, some or all of the staff had received in-service training in the year prior to our visit. Such training had occurred in 48 per cent of Local Authority homes, 51 per cent of Health Authority homes and in 42 per cent of the voluntary homes. In the private sector, however, only 17 per cent of the homes had provided such training. In all the agencies, staff were sent to other training courses and it is notable, as Table 4.9 indicates, that 46 per cent of the private homes' staff had been sent on such courses. However, the private sector also produced the highest number of homes (33 per cent) without any training occurring for staff in the 12 months prior to our visit.

Table 4.9 Percentage of homes providing training for staff in the preceding 12 months

Agency	In-service Training	CSS/Post-basic Nursing	Other Training	No Training	No Information
Local Authority	48	17	26	7	2
Health Authority	51	20	20	7	2
Private Sector	17	4	46	33	–
Voluntary Sector	42	–	42	12	4
Overall	43	13	30	12	2

Staff Meetings

Staff meetings occurred in the majority of public sector homes and in the voluntary homes but only in a small number of private homes. Staff meetings were held in 95 per cent of Local Authority homes, 88 per cent of Health Authority homes, 85 per cent of voluntary homes and 63 per cent of private homes. However, the frequency of these meetings varied considerably, as Table 4.10 indicates. Staff meetings did not occur very often; in the majority of homes in all agencies they were held less often than weekly.

Table 4.10 Frequency of staff meetings in homes in all four agencies

Agency	Daily	Weekly	Monthly	Less Often
Local Authority	2	27	52	20
Health Authority	13	26	45	16
Private Sector*	27	27	–	7
Voluntary Sector	–	48	44	9
Overall	7	31	47	15

*No meetings held in 7 per cent of the homes.

Delegation of Authority to Staff

Four indicators of staff autonomy were obtained.

1. The scale of staff autonomy

This scale consists of 11 items, each rated on a three-point scale. The details about the construction of this scale were described in Chapter 1. The range of scores on this scale is from 11 to 33, with the higher score representing maximum autonomy in decision making by the first-line manager in the home.

Data were available for 43 Local Authority, 29 Health Authority and 15 voluntary sector homes. The private sector homes were excluded because delegation would, by definition, be in the hands of the owners of these facilities. The responses of the owners interviewed indicated this to be the case. Table 4.11 shows the mean scores for the homes in each of the agency types.

Table 4.11 Mean scores on the Staff Autonomy Scale by agency type

Agency	Mean SAS Score	s.d.	No. of Cases
Local Authority	27.56	2.25	43
Health Authority	27.83	2.66	29
Voluntary Sector	28.27	2.80	15
Overall	27.80	2.50	87

There was a significant difference between the groups on this scale (F=24.5, d.f.=3, 86 p<.001).

2. Control of temperature within the homes

The temperature of the homes was controlled in 20 per cent of Local Authority homes and 17 per cent of Health Authority homes by central services. Thus alterations to the thermostat within the home had to be done by contacting the central service agency, usually the engineer's department. This was the case in one voluntary home.

3. The daily menu

In the majority of homes the daily menus were planned by first-line managers. However, in 21 per cent of Local Authorities and 13 per cent of Health Authorities, as compared to only 8 per cent of the voluntary homes, the daily menu was either controlled by a central catering department or by cooks in the facility and not by the first-line managers in the homes.

4. Financial control

Facilities were classified according to the extent to which financial responsibility was delegated or otherwise in the hands of the person with day-to-day operational responsibility. A five-fold classification was used.

- A=Centralized system. No control over resource use other than small items from petty cash. Authority needed for the purchase of large items. Everyday provisions to be ordered and supplied from central stores or through bulk contracts.
- B=Cost centre. Budget devolved to facility and officer in charge is informed regularly of expenditure. Some discretion over source of supplies though transactions are usually made under contract and billed to managing agency.
- C=Imprest system. Cash allowance given for household items with complete discretion over how this is spent.
- D=Entrepreneurial system. As in the private sector where single cash allowance (fee) covers all resource needs. Complete discretion over how this is allocated between resources.
- E= Independent living. Resident retains control over spending decisions on household items funded usually from welfare benefit.

The results are shown in Table 4.12.

Table 4.12 Percentage of facilities by degree of financial control

Agency	A	B	C	D	E	No. of Cases
Local Authority	37	33	9	–	21	57
Health Authority	15	12	37	–	37	41
Private Sector	–	–	–	100	–	24
Voluntary Sector	8	–	46	27	19	26
TOTAL	20	16	22	21	22	148

Amongst the statutory agencies, Health Authorities had taken advantage (or perhaps made a virtue of necessity) of smaller domestic-size units and delegated much financial responsibility down to first-line managers through the use of imprest systems. However, there were notable exceptions to this, such as the Local Authority facility which had enabled some residents to become tenants of what was effectively a large hostel. The residents paid a small rent for their room, heating and lighting but retained much of their social security benefits to purchase food and clothing.

The consequences of financial delegation on the costs and quality of the service provided and on the staff who must bear the responsibility have been explored by Shiell *et al.* (1992). The tentative conclusion offered from this analysis was that managers of residential facilities would welcome the devolution of budgets and this would contribute to more effective and efficient use of resources.

Staff Monitoring

To consider monitoring at all it is first necessary to establish whether homes have philosophies with goals and aims staff are meant to implement. The majority of homes we visited did have such philosophies but there were clear differences between agencies here. Table 4.13 shows the percentage of homes with statements of philosophies.

Table 4.13 Homes with statements of philosophy

Agency	No. of Homes	Per cent
Local Authority	20	35
Health Authority	31	76
Private Sector	15	65
Voluntary Sector	16	58
Overall	82	55

The existence of written statements of philosophy was highest in Health Authority homes and lowest in Local Authority homes.

We asked if any checklists of standards were used by facility managers to monitor care practices in each of the homes. Table 4.14 presents the results. Very few facilities used the National Development Group's Checklist of Standards for Improving the Quality of Services for Mentally Handicapped People (National Development Group, 1980). Rather more facilities made use of the PASS rating system or some other checklist such as Home Life˙ (Avebury, 1984). Less than half of the facilities in all agencies used such tools to assess the quality of the service they provided. Irrespective of agency, routine monitoring of the quality of service delivery is not part of the culture of many homes.

Table 4.14 Percentage of homes using checklists of standards to monitor quality of service

Agency	NDG	PASS	Other Checklist	None*
Local Authority	12	28	16	52
Health Authority	17	34	13	56
Private Sector	13	25	8	58
Voluntary Sector	4	23	23	54
Overall	12	28	15	54

*Totals will not add to 100 per cent because some homes use more than one checklist.

Chapter 5

Characteristics of People in Residential Care

Personal Characteristics

Age

The mean age of residents was very similar across all sectors. In Health and Local Authority homes the mean age was 39 years and it was 41 years in voluntary and private homes.

Sex

There were proportionately more males than females in homes in all sectors. The highest proportion of males (60 per cent) lived in voluntary homes and the lowest proportion (52 per cent) in Local Authority homes. In private and Health Authority homes, 55 per cent of residents were male.

Previous Homes

Previous homes of residents are shown in Table 5.1

The effects of care in the community policies can be seen in the number of admissions to community-based homes from mental handicap hospitals (35 per cent). The NHS homes admitted 71 per cent of their residents from this source. This follows the findings of the PSSRU/CHE survey of private and voluntary residential and nursing homes (Darton *et al.*, 1993) in which 76 per cent of private homes and 60 per cent of voluntary homes reported receiving referrals from hospitals. Parents also acted as main sources of referral for residents in Local Authority (39 per cent), private (21 per cent) and voluntary homes (33 per cent). In the PSSRU/CHE survey, 45 per cent of private and 16 per cent of voluntary homes received referrals from relatives.

Table 5.1 Previous homes of residents

	Current Residence									
	NHS		Local Authority		Private Sector		Voluntary Sector		All	
Previous Home	No.	%	No.	%	No.	%	No.	%	No.	%
Hospital	163	71	162	23	94	46	41	24	460	35
NHS Community Unit	13	6	11	2	3	2	3	2	30	2
Parents	38	17	282	39	43	21	55	33	418	32
Own Home	3	1	27	4	11	5	11	7	52	4
Foster Home	2	1	5	1	1	<1	3	2	11	1
Lodgings	0	0	4	1	1	<1	4	2	9	1
LA Hostel	1	<1	123	17	14	7	14	8	152	12
Min. Staff LA Home	1	<1	13	2	8	4	0	0	22	2
LA Group Home	3	1	33	5	2	1	4	2	42	3
Private	0	0	7	1	9	4	4	2	20	2
Voluntary	0	0	5	1	4	2	11	7	20	2
Housing Association	0	0	1	<1	0	0	2	<1	3	<1
Other	5	2	45	6	16	8	16	10	82	6
Not Known	0	0	3	<1	0	0	0	0	3	<1
TOTAL	229		721		206		168		1324	

Medical Needs

Most residents (81 per cent) were reported to have no serious medical needs. There were 18 residents (1 per cent) who had 24-hour medical care needs and nine of these were in NHS facilities. Another 24 residents (2 per cent) had life-threatening conditions of whom 16 were in Local Authority homes.

Table 5.2 Medical needs of residents

	NHS		Local Authority		Private Sector		Voluntary Sector		All	
	No.	%	No.	%	No.	%	No.	%	No.	%
No serious needs	177	78	579	81	178	84	139	82	1083	81
Regular visits needed	36	16	122	17	30	14	25	15	213	16
Life-threatening	4	2	16	2	1	<1	3	2	24	2
24-hour medical needs	9	4	2	<1	4	2	3	2	18	1
TOTAL	226		719		213		170		1328	

Presence of Impairments and Conditions

Facilities administered by Health Authorities had the largest proportion of residents with physical handicap and with the sensory impairments of deafness and blindness (Table 5.3). In addition, those facilities also had the greatest proportion of people suffering from cerebral palsy or epilepsy. All facilities had a fairly large proportion (45 per cent) of residents with behavioural disorders. It was noticeable that the private homes had the greatest proportion of people with behavioural disorders (54 per cent) or with mental illness (18 per cent). All 13 residents in one private home displayed challenging behaviour and all 16 residents in one voluntary home were autistic. In addition, three private homes were dually registered as residential and nursing homes and accommodated people with mental illness as well as people with learning disabilities.

Adaptive Behaviour Scores of Residents

Information on the personal behaviour of residents was collected in a form using the Behaviour Development Survey (BDS) which is an abbreviated and adapted version (Conroy, 1980) of the Adaptive Behaviour Scale (Nihira, 1976). This scale has two main indexes, one relating to adaptive behaviour and the other to maladaptive behaviour. The first index consists of three factors – personal self-sufficiency; community self-sufficiency and personal/social responsibility – but there is a good case for treating these three factors as an index rather than as separate domains (Arndt, 1981). The scores along this index range from 0 to 128 and higher scores denote higher

Table 5.3 Number and proportion of residents with certain impairments and conditions

Agency	Physical Handicap n	%	Deafness n	%	Blindness n	%	Autism n	%	Cerebral Palsy n	%	Epilepsy n	%	Mental Illness n	%	Behavioural Disorders n	%	Other Disorders n	%
NHS	211	41	198	12	197	11	192	7	235	10	235	37	234	12	208	44	235	22
Local Authority	657	17	641	6	649	6	636	6	735	2	738	20	736	12	666	44	737	17
Private	184	17	174	9	177	8	175	15	216	2	216	21	215	18	190	56	216	24
Voluntary	156	13	156	8	155	4	158	10	172	1	172	13	172	11	157	34	172	13
TOTAL	1208	21	1169	8	1178	7	1161	8	1358	3	1361	22	1357	13	1221	45	1360	19

behavioural competence. The scores for residents from the facilities in each sector are set out in Table 5.4.

Table 5.4 Adaptive behaviour scores

Score	NHS No.	%	Local Authority No.	%	Private Sector No.	%	Voluntary Sector No.	%	All No.	%
14-50	67	33	60	10	32	18	4	3	163	15
51-75	38	19	109	18	49	27	25	18	221	20
76-100	53	26	209	34	58	31	49	36	369	33
101-128	45	22	206	38	44	24	60	43	355	32
Total	203		584		183		138		1108	
Mean Score	66.7		87.2		78.1		93.2		82.7	
s.d.	37.4		25.5		28.3		21.3		29.3	

The analysis of variance showed there was a significant difference in the distribution of behavioural competence in the residents in the different residential settings (F=33.0, df = 3, 1104 p=<0.001). The residents in Health Authority facilities had the lowest behavioural competence; those in voluntary facilities had the highest competence.

Chapter 6

The Costs of Community Residential Provision

Summary

- Average costs (1987-8 prices) across all community facilities were £38 per resident-day.
- Costs ranged from £16 per resident-day to £95 per resident-day.
- On average health service facilities were the most expensive, independent sector facilities the least expensive.
- Services provided by other agencies add between 15 and 25 per cent to the accounted costs of residential provision.
- Dependency was positively correlated with costs only in the statutory sector. In independent sector facilities there was no relationship between dependency and cost.
- Economies of scale were not apparent in facilities larger than six places. In smaller facilities, the effect of size on costs was unclear, clouded by other factors such as the dependency of clients.
- Differences in the characteristics of clients (age and disability level) were the most important factors which explained differences in the cost of residential services.
- Facility characteristics such as the number of places, the type of building, the range of services provided, the internal layout and environmental quality were not significantly related to costs.
- A composite quality of service measure was positively associated with costs.
- Costs were lower in private and voluntary homes even when allowing for differences in residents' characteristics and the quality of care.
- These conclusions are dependent on the representativeness of the private sector participants and the extent to which the dependency measure employed in the analysis actually picks up differences in the capabilities of clients.

Costs

The average cost across all 125 facilities for which information on each component of cost was available was £38 per resident-day (1987-8 prices). Average daily costs ranged from £16 to £95 per resident and as Table 6.1 shows, there are large differences between the agencies. Facilities in the independent sector are markedly less expensive than either of the two statutory agencies (ANOVA: F=11.296, d.f. = 3, p<0.001).

Table 6.1 Mean costs per day

Agency	Mean Cost £	s.d. £	Range £
Local Authority	37.20	12.70	16.50 – 91.70
Health Authority	49.00	19.70	19.00 – 94.70
Private Sector	27.80	8.40	19.90 – 60.50
Voluntary Sector	32.40	10.60	16.00 – 59.40
All Facilities	38.20	15.90	16.00 – 94.70

A breakdown of these costs into their component elements also revealed interesting differences between the providing agencies (see Table 6.2). Staffing and non-staff costs made up those elements which are usually included in the budget of statutory facilities and which, together with capital, made up the costs to be met from fee-income of private sector homes. Staff and non-staff expenditures comprised a much larger proportion of the total costs of Health Authority facilities. This reflected their greater propensity to provide 24-hour care to the residents instead of using day services provided by other agencies. There were differences in the overall levels of costs of Local Authority and voluntary sector homes and in the balance between staff and non-staff costs, but if these two elements of cost are considered together, the proportions of expenditure on each major category of resource use are almost identical.

In terms of proportionate expenditures, private sector facilities fell somewhere in between Health and Local Authority facilities. This is a reflection of the relationship between private sector providers and Local Authority-run day services. In some areas, private sector residents were denied access to social education centres because they had not previously lived in the area or simply because they lived in privately run homes. In the latter case, the argument used in justification was that the income support payment was meant to cover 24-hour care including day services. The owners of other private sector homes chose to make their own day services arrangements because of concerns about the quality of day care provided by social services. As a result, day services comprised a smaller proportion of total costs in private sector homes compared to Local Authority or voluntary provision, though it is not as small as in Health Authority facilities.

Table 6.2 Components of daily cost

Cost Component	Percentage of Daily Cost by Agency			
	LA	HA	Pte	Vol
Staff	53	65	84	46
Non-staff	19	20	*	28
Day services	16	7	13	16
Volunteers	<1	<1	1	<1
Domiciliary	3	2	2	2
Capital	8	5	*	8
TOTAL (£)	37.20	49.00	27.80	32.35

*These costs are included in 'staff'.

The differences in the proportion of costs directly accounted to each facility reinforces the need to be consistent when compiling cost estimates. Considering only those costs which are directly attributed to residential facilities would cause one to neglect between 15 and 25 per cent of the total cost of community-based residential accommodation and would distort comparisons of the relative costs of services provided by different agencies.

Costs and Dependency

The differences in costs between agencies was due, in part, to the characteristics of the people living in homes provided by each sector. Levels of social and personal functioning, as measured by the Behaviour Development Survey (Conroy, 1980) were higher in the independent sector compared to the statutory sector and higher in

Local Authority homes than in Health Authority facilities (see Chapter 5). Dependency was positively related to costs overall and for both statutory agencies separately but not for private or voluntary sector homes (see Tables 6.3 and 6.4). The absence of any relationship between costs and dependency in the independent sector is not surprising since the level of income support payments, on which charges and therefore costs tended to be based, was fixed and not related to client need.

Table 6.3 Relationship between costs and personal self-sufficiency (BDS)

Mean BDS Score	Mean Cost per Day (£)
0 – 29	68.50
30 – 59	46.90
60 – 89	37.20
90 – 120	30.40

Note: Higher scores on the BDS denote higher levels of personal and social functioning.

Table 6.4 Correlation between costs and dependency

Agency	Pearson Correlation Coefficient	Significance
Local Authority	0.406	0.006
Health Authority	0.650	0.001
Private Sector	0.070	0.770
Voluntary Sector	0.177	0.469
All Facilities	0.593	0.001

Costs and Size

Average costs per resident were negatively correlated with the size of facilities for the sample overall and in the Local Authorities, Health Authorities and the voluntary sector, if the agencies are considered separately. However, as Table 6.5 shows, the relationship is not significant at conventional levels for either the Health Authority or the voluntary sector. The significant positive relationship between costs and size in the private sector is interesting for it suggests that, other things being equal, small private sector facilities were less expensive to run. In one respect, this may be true. The owners of smaller facilities provide a greater proportion of the staff input themselves. By taking a smaller return should fee-income (set at income support levels) prove inadequate, they have greater scope to keep costs down. However, the positive relationship found here is most likely an artifact of our data. One large private sector facility stood out from the rest by having costs in excess of £60 per day. Referring Local Authorities topped up the residents' social security payments to meet the fees of £400 – £500 per week because the facility provided an extensive range of residential, day time and educational services for young adults. If this 'outlier' is removed from the analysis, the correlation between costs and size in the private sector remains positive but is no longer statistically significant.

The analysis shown in Table 6.5 assumes there is a simple linear relationship between costs and the size of facilities. Economies of scale are better represented by a more complex 'U-shaped' or an 'L-shaped' relationship. Simple observation of the scatter of points often indicates which sort of relationship is most appropriate. In this case, the wide variation in costs among facilities of similar size means that this approach is not very illuminating. Any of a number of relationships (linear, U- or L-shaped) could be fitted to the scatter of points depending on the weight given to facilities with extreme values of cost.

Table 6.5 Correlations between average costs per day and size of facilities

Agency	Pearson Correlation Coefficient	Significance
Local Authority	–0.355	0.006
Health Authority	–0.054	0.380
Private Sector	0.534	0.008
Voluntary Sector	–0.297	0.102
All Facilities	–0.184	0.021

The sensitivity of the relationship between cost and size to different treatment of outlying facilities is best illustrated by considering an example. This is a Health Authority facility located in a new purpose-built unit comprising three neighbouring bungalows, each of which has six residents. If the management of this facility had been organized differently, it could just as easily have been classified for the purposes of this study as three separate units. In this case, an L-shaped relationship between cost and size would seem as appropriate as any other, with the junction of the two axes occurring somewhere around six or eight places. In facilities larger than six places, the line of best fit between cost and size would be almost horizontal (albeit with a wide margin of error on either side) suggesting there were little or no economies of scale in large facilities. In facilities with fewer than six places, the relationship between cost and size appears almost vertical, which may suggest there are sharp increases in costs per resident as one reduces the size of facilities. This observation is supported by preliminary findings from the NIMROD project in Wales which found little difference in the total costs of supporting four people in a house from the total cost of supporting six people (Davies *et al.*, 1990).

However, this speculation assumes other things are held constant which is obviously not the case. Any relationship found here is possibly as much to do with different levels of dependency amongst the residents of small houses as it is due to technical factors related to scale. This point is explored more fully in the next section.

Costs, Size and Dependency

The relationship between the size of facilities and cost is difficult to determine because of the confounding effects of dependency. The greatest variation in cost occurred in the smaller facilities. Here, the practice of accommodating people of similar levels of disability together in the one house has the effect of polarizing the average costs. In larger facilities, costs associated with the higher dependency of some residents are cancelled out by the lesser needs of more-able residents. In the seven most expensive facilities, costs per resident-day exceeded £60. Six of these were Health Authority facilities, three of which were established as a result of a Department of Health financial initiative aimed at getting severely handicapped children out of hospital (Leonard, 1987). Two other small domestic-scale facilities, also established as a result of this initiative, had costs in excess of £50 per resident-day. Five of the seven high-cost facilities were located in ordinary domestic housing stock with five or fewer residents, and two were in newly constructed units built to a similar design as each other with three bungalows on the same site. One of these had 18 residents in three blocks of six, the other had 24 residents in three blocks of eight.

At the other extreme, there were 16 facilities (all also small in scale) in which residents were so independent that no night-staff were required and only a minimal staff input was needed during the day, usually to assist with budgeting, meal preparation or social programmes. In these facilities, non-staff expenditures were paid for by the residents directly out of social security entitlements. Average costs in the 12 houses for which costs could be calculated totalled less than £25 per resident-day.

Some idea of the relationship between size of facility, the characteristics of residents and cost can be obtained from Table 6.6 which groups together facilities according to dependency and number of places. 'Independent living' describes those facilities which have no night-staff on site; 'domestic' relates to facilities with six or fewer places that do have night-staff; and 'high dependency' describes facilities in which the average score on the BDS is below 30. On average, independent living facilities were one-half of the cost of similar size facilities for people of medium dependency and one-third of the cost of similar size facilities for people of high dependency.

Table 6.6 Costs per day by type of facility

Facility Type (No.)	Mean Cost	s.d.
Independent Living (12)	23.70	5.40
Domestic/High Dependency (6)	74.80	16.20
Other/High Dependency (2)	60.50	–
Domestic/Medium dependency (19)	49.60	17.10
Medium Size/Medium Dependency (28)	31.50	8.60
Large Size/Medium Dependency (19)	33.10	11.40
Purpose-built/Not Subdivided (18)	38.50	11.90
Purpose-built/Subdivided (21)	36.00	8.30

Comparing the costs of the remaining facilities which accommodate people with similar, though broadly measured, levels of social and personal skills, there was little difference between medium-size and larger facilities but the cost of domestic-scale accommodation is much higher. If economies of scale exist, a cut-off point at about six places is suggested. Indeed, if purpose-built units were to be included there may be diseconomies in large facilities. However, this type of accommodation was used mainly by Local Authorities and the effect is more likely due to higher average levels of dependency in such facilities than to the type of facility *per se*.

Analysis of Variations in Costs

Model specification

Theoretically, costs are a function both of input prices and the rate of output. For community living facilities, the number of resident-days is the primary output, but differences in quality of care between facilities mean that this output is not homogeneous. In addition, residential care is not the sole output and facilities might also provide day services and respite care. Residential facilities are therefore better characterized as multi-product firms providing a range of services for different sorts of client.

The general model of residential facility costs tested here suggests that the average cost of each facility depends upon its capacity and rate of utilization, the mix of services provided, the physical characteristics of the facility, the quality of service provided and the characteristics of the residents. There is no readily available index of regional costs for the UK, therefore the costs of factor inputs has had to be dropped from the analysis. Fortunately, there is little *a priori* evidence to suggest that factor prices differ by very much across the country once one excludes London.

Variable specification

Many of the variables listed in Table 6.7 are self-evident or have been described in previous sections.

In addition to measures of quality described in Chapter 1, a single 'structural' measure based on the physical environment of each facility (OREQY) was constructed. This was based on the researchers' impressions of the domesticity of the home environment and its immediate surroundings. In previous work, little correlation has been found between these dimensions, and facilities might score highly on one measure of quality but not on others. The scales, therefore, appeared to measure different dimensions of care. In preliminary analysis of our data, high correlations were found between each of the four indicators of process, quality of care. Rather than analyse these quality variables separately (which would lead to co-linearity) a composite variable was created by factor analysis. This identified two factors, one relating to the physical environment comprising the OREQY variable and one which combined the four measures of process quality. The factor weights of this composite variable were used in the subsequent cost function analysis as a single process-quality of care variable (labelled QUALITY).

Table 6.7 List of variables and brief description

DEPENDENT VARIABLE

| COSTDAY | Total cost per resident-day |

INDEPENDENT VARIABLES

Capacity and Utilization

PLACES	Number of available places per day
SQPLACES	Places squared
OCCUP	Average percentage occupancy per day
SQOCCUP	Occupancy squared
RESPITE	Percentage of places for respite care
DAYSERV	Equals 1 if day services provided on site

Physical Characteristics of Facility

BUILT	Equals 1 if purpose-built
DIVIDED	Equals 1 if subdivided into smaller units
AGENCY1	Equals 1 if managed by Local Authority
AGENCY2	Equals 1 if managed by Health Authority
AGENCY3	Equals 1 if for-profit
OREQY	Indicator of physical quality of facility

Quality of Service

IPDL	Index of participation in domestic living
GHMS	Group home management scale
IAA	Index of adult autonomy
ICI	Index of community involvement
QUALRAT	Proportion of qualified staff

Characteristics of Residents

AGE	Average age of residents
SQAGE	Age squared
BDS	Average score on Behaviour Development Survey
STAY	Average length of stay of long-term residents

Functional form

With the exception of quadratic terms to allow for non-linear effects particularly in relation to size, there is little *a priori* evidence to indicate the most appropriate functional form. In preliminary analysis, a simple linear-in-parameters functional form was found to perform just as well when measured in terms of adjusted R^2 as semi-log or log linear models. Only the results for the additive-linear model are presented here.

The choice of dependent variable is also not without problem. Vitaliano (1987) argues that total cost is to be preferred on econometric grounds because average costs, by including outcome measures on both sides of the equation, may cause bias. However, in a review of the specification of hospital cost functions, Breyer (1987) argues that using total cost also has serious econometric drawbacks. As our objective is to explain differences in the cost per unit of output of residential facilities, it seems more appropriate to use cost per resident-day as the dependent variable. The PLACES and SQPLACES variable will then trace the long-run average costs while the OCCUPANCY variables will trace short-run deviations.

Results

Mean scores on the quality variables are shown by agency in Table 6.8. In all cases, the results have been scaled to score 0–30, with higher scores indicating better quality. Significant differences were found amongst facilities. Those run by the independent sector were more attractive and provided more individualized accommodation than statutory facilities. In private sector facilities, clients were less likely to be involved in activities relating to daily domestic tasks and care regimes were less individually-orientated that homes in other sectors. Opportunities for clients to make decisions about their own lives were infrequent in all homes but Local Authority homes and voluntary homes provided the most opportunity to do this and private sector homes the least. The use of generic community amenities was uniformly low in all facilities.

Table 6.8 Mean scores on quality indicators

Agency	OREQY	GHMS	IAA	ICI	IPDL
Local Authority	17.2	18.1	18.5	12.7	17.8
Health Authority	19.8	17.8	14.5	12.7	19.3
Private Sector	23.7	12.6	16.0	12.8	21.8
Voluntary Sector	24.8	18.3	18.5	14.9	15.5
ANOVA	(0.001)	(0.02)	(0.001)	(NS)	(0.001)

Note: All scales score 0–30; high scores indicate better quality of service for all indicators except the IPDL.

The results of the multiple regression analysis are shown in Table 6.9. The simple-additive model is able to explain 65 per cent (as measured by adjusted R^2) of the variation in costs between facilities, which for cross-sectional data, is more than satisfactory.

Seven of the coefficients reached statistical significance at conventional levels and two more (including the intercept) were significant at the 90 per cent level. The physical structure of the building and the quality of the physical environment had no effect on cost. The hypothesis that costs are related to size of facility must also be rejected on this evidence. Neither coefficient on PLACES or SQPLACES reaches statistical significance at acceptable levels and, perhaps as a result, the signs are the opposite of those required to describe the traditional 'U-shaped' average cost curve.

Occupancy rates usually affect average costs because it is not easy to vary the resources used with the number of residents and, therefore, low occupancy rates usually produce higher average cost per resident. The absence of any significant relationship between occupancy and average cost in this analysis was probably due to the lack of variation in occupancy between facilities. All facilities aimed to provide long-term accommodation and there was little turnover of permanent residents. Respite beds comprised only a small proportion of the total places in each facility and, where provided, were always used intensively. Overall percentage occupancy was, with only one or two exceptions, universally high.

The significance of the QUALRAT variable is interesting. This variable measures the proportion of all staff (in full-time equivalents) who have professional nursing or social work qualifications. The

Table 6.9 Regression coefficients

	B	SE B	Sign	
Constant	127.536	68.821	0.068	*
Agency 1	8.570	3.583	0.019	**
Agency 2	9.230	3.637	0.013	**
Agency 2	−2.307	3.684	0.533	
BUILT	−1.205	2.869	0.676	
DIVIDED	0.034	3.057	0.991	
RESPITE	−0.079	0.104	0.450	
DAYSERV	−3.477	2.487	0.166	
PLACES	0.586	0.816	0.475	
SQPLACES	−0.018	0.024	0.449	
OCCUP	0.234	1.552	0.881	
SQOCCUP	−0.003	0.009	0.755	
BDS	−0.353	0.100	0.001	***
AGE	−2.490	0.493	0.000	***
SQAGE	0.024	0.005	0.000	***
STAY	−0.038	0.018	0.031	**
QUALRAT	−13.764	6.801	0.046	**
QUALITY	4.477	2.530	0.081	*
OREQY	0.327	1.219	0.789	
Analysis of	Variance	DF	R^2	0.647
	Regression	18	F	11.122
	Residual	81		(sig^n F=0.000)

*	significant at 90 per cent
**	significant at 95 per cent
***	significant at 99 per cent

indication that average cost per resident is lower where the proportion of qualified staff is greater suggests that there is an efficiency effect from employing more qualified staff.

Of the client characteristics, both AGE and SQAGE are highly significant, with the signs on the coefficients indicating that younger residents and older residents tended to cost more to accommodate than those in middle age. The average length of stay of the residents was also significant and indicates that facilities in which residents were more established tend to be less expensive. As would be expected, greater personal and social self-sufficiency is related to lower average costs.

The AGENCY variables relate to the costs of voluntary (ie, not for profit, non-statutory) providers. Private, for-profit facilities were cheaper though not significantly so. Residents of private and voluntary sector homes relied predominantly on income support payments to pay their fees. The fee-income of independent sector providers (and the potential expenditure of such homes) is closely related to the level at which income support limits are set. It is therefore not surprising that there is little difference in cost per day between private and voluntary sector providers. Local Authority and Health Authority facilities were significantly more expensive than those in the independent sector even after differences in the quality of care and the characteristics of residents have been taken into account.

Finally, the coefficient on the composite of QUALITY variable was positive and significant at the 90 per cent level. The result indicates that facilities which were more client-orientated and integrated with their local community were also more expensive to run.

Discussion

The overall aim of British government policy is (or at least should be) more cost-effective care in the community. In practice, two distinct elements of policy can be discerned from government statements. The first is a shift towards smaller residential facilities; the second is the development of a mixed economy of care with less reliance on public provision. The findings of this study would appear to confirm that both strands of policy are contributing to the achievement of the desired aim. Smaller facilities of four to six places appeared no more expensive than larger ones, and independent sector provision appeared to be cheaper than statutory provision, even after differences in the characteristics of residents and the quality of care are controlled. However, for a number of reasons, these findings should be interpreted with caution.

Though the statistical analysis indicates no significant relationship between size and cost, which suggest there are no economies of scale to be lost by providing care in smaller units, simple observation of the scatter of points between costs and the number of places suggests that costs rise quickly if there are less than four places in a facility. These results need further testing but they are consistent with experience in other small community residential schemes in the United Kingdom (Davies *et al.*, 1990).

The relationship between agency type and cost is similarly more complicated than it appears. If the sample of private residential facilities is representative (and it should be emphasized that it may not be) *and* differences in the quality of care and the characteristics of residents are accurately reflected in the composite quality variable and the BDS score respectively, then the relationship detected here arose from relative inefficiency in the statutory sector. However, there were distinct differences in the type of resident accommodated by the different agencies, with Health Authority facilities catering for the most dependent and the private and voluntary providers dealing with the most independent. As a measure of dependency, the BDS score has a number of shortcomings. It may give insufficient weight to degrees of incapacity and, in the form used here, it does not measure maladaptive or challenging behaviour. The agency variables may therefore be picking up differences in the characteristics of residents which are not totally captured by the BDS. In addition, the relationships detected here may be partly the result of the BDS score being highly correlated with the individual measures of quality.

Our results also suggest that better quality of care, as indicated by the composite quality construct, contributed to higher costs. This may seem self-evident but the relationship is not as clear as it first appears. The separate quality measures which make up the composite variable are concerned with the manner in which staff relate to residents and the opportunities residents have to make decisions about everyday aspects of their lives and to use community facilities. There are no obvious reasons why these factors should have any direct effect on costs.

The use of process measures of quality assumes that improvements in the quality of service are so called because they have a beneficial impact on client well-being or utility. This assumption seems plausible but nevertheless remains an assumption which should be tested. If it can be shown to be valid and the positive relationship between cost and quality of care holds, then it is for policy makers to decide whether subsequent improvements in the quality of care are worth the additional cost. This requires a comparison of the value of improvements in the quality of community care with the marginal value of the outcomes likely to be obtained from those activities with which community service must compete for resources. Community care is funded from the health and social services budget so these other activities will, in large part, comprise acute medical services. The breadth of coverage of the quality measures used here to evaluate community care suggests that whatever impact it has on client welfare, it will go beyond the changes in health state recorded in the most widely used generic measure (Kind *et al.*, 1982; Sackett and Torrance, 1978) and will include factors such as self-esteem and fulfilment of potential, as well as more material concerns relating to the physical appearance of one's living space. The objectives of residential provision are broader than the maintenance or improvement of physical or mental health and so it is important to consider these other dimensions of outcome when comparing the efficient use of resources.

Chapter 7
Policy Implications

Introduction

As stated in Chapter 1, the research was carried out amidst continuing debate on the objectives, principles and values of residential care. Following the recommendations of the Wagner Committee (1988), there is growing acceptance of the principles of 'ordinary living' for people with learning disabilities. Many of these principles are contained in the so-called 'five accomplishments' set out by O'Brien (1987) and listed in Chapter 1. The main values in these accomplishments are concerned with allowing or facilitating people with learning disabilities to have control and choice over their relationships, life-styles, and daily living routines, to be compensated in a dignified way for any disability they suffer and to participate in the general life of their local communities. The research was able to assess how well these principles are being put into operation in different managing agencies and with varying cost consequences.

It must be remembered, however, that the survey covered a representative sample of homes in England (outside the Inner London area) and therefore included many homes which were built or converted well before many of the present principles were outlined or accepted. Consequently, we would expect to find a varied picture on the achievement of the objectives set for 'ordinary living'. There has also been a dramatic policy shift in the provision of residential care as a result of a long debate, (Audit Commission, 1986; Griffiths, 1987) a government White Paper (DoH, 1989) and the resulting National Health Service and Community Care Act, 1990.

So far as residential care for people with learning disabilities is concerned, the main implications of the new arrangements are:

- Income support payments which were used to finance residents in the independent sector's homes have been transferred to Local Authorities.

- Local Authorities are responsible for assessing the care and financial needs of people entering residential care after April 1993.

- Local Authorities are to take a role as enablers rather than providers of care.

- Local Authorities must make full use of the independent sector. They have two main incentives to do this: 85 per cent of the money transferred from the social security budget is to be spent in the independent sector; and the Local Authority will contribute more to the cost of people cared for in its own homes than in homes in the independent sector.

- Local Authorities have already or are now in the process of transferring their own homes to the voluntary sector as a result of the financial rules outlined in the point immediately above.

- Local Authorities retain their powers to inspect and enforce standards of care in residential homes and to specify in their contracts with providers of residential care the quality of the services they expect for clients.

Policy Implications

The main findings of the research provide encouraging pointers to the achievement of good quality of care. The findings reported in Chapter 3 show that progress has been made in several aspects of care, although some of the historical legacy of the 1970s developments are still present. Homes in the independent sector and the NHS were much more likely than Local Authority homes to be in medium or large housing stock, although both public sector agencies had more small, domestic-scale provision than the private sector. The private sector homes were, however, much less likely than other homes to be within a concentrated set of services for disabled people.

Given that it takes time to shift the distribution of size of homes from the large (over 20 places) to smaller, domestic-scale units, it is not surprising that one of the points which emerged from the survey was that residents were not closely integrated into their local communities. As stated in Chapter 3, few residents in *many* homes had much contact with friends in the community and the use of community facilities was uniformly low in all sectors. The majority of residents went on holiday with people from their own home rather than with relatives or friends from outside the home.

The integration of residents with other members of the community is closely linked to policies on day services. Considerable encouragement is being given to day service providers to move away from specific facilities such as the large social education centres to the use of schools, colleges, leisure complexes, swimming pools and recreation halls within the community (Social Services Inspectorate, 1989). Again, this change in policy will take time to implement, so people in residential care will tend to receive the day services which are provided locally and integration will change at the same pace as the local provision. As Local Authorities change their organizations to be enablers or purchasers rather than providers of care, specific facilities will be costed and charged for by the new providers. Given the move to transfer ownership of homes out of the Local Authorities to the independent sector, new initiatives are likely to encourage the shift away from the large day centres to the use of general facilities.

The acceptance of the principles of ordinary living would seem to favour the use of 'ordinary' housing stock for newly established residential homes. Certainly, this would aid integration in the community, but it is not certain to increase the homeliness or individualization of care. These attributes depend on the routine established within the home. The results of the survey reported in Chapter 3 showed that there was still room for improving these aspects of the quality of care. Part of this is reflected in the design and layout of homes, and given the historical legacy of the public sector, it is not very surprising to find that voluntary and private sector homes were more attractive and provided more individualized accommodation than the public sector homes. However, giving residents choice and control over the home's routines is not dependent on the physical layout of the building. Although there was evidence that in a majority of homes residents had choice over bed times and getting up, main mealtimes tended to be early and present little opportunity for flexibility of choice. The scoring on the scale which measured the extent to which residents had choice and control over daily routines was also rather low in all provider groups. In other scales which tested residents' opportunities for choices and management of their daily lives, the Local Authority homes scored better than homes provided by the NHS or private sector, despite the worries expressed earlier about the size and location of Local Authority homes. This evidence reinforces the point that the philosophy of care can lead to good quality care if the staff are encouraged to accept and practise it.

A considerable responsibility for improving the quality of residential care now lies with the inspection units in Local Authorities and the purchasing arm of social services departments. This research shows that there are useful scales or even single questions which would enable inspectors to make baseline assessments and to check or monitor changes in the quality of care. The evidence on the quality of processes of care, homeliness and individualization of care, suggests that although the type, size and location of homes may well be important in achieving objectives of care concerned with community integration, these factors should not prevent managers or owners from establishing principles which ensure that residents have every opportunity to receive care which meets their individual needs and rights to lead as full a life as possible with all due dignity, privacy and appropriate compensation for disability.

The evidence from the costing studies reinforces the conclusions on the quality of care evidence. There was evidence that better quality of care is related to higher costs per resident, but there was little evidence that costs increased as the size of homes decreased except, possibly, for homes with less than four to six residents. This is generally in line with other studies which have noted the costs of caring for people in homes with two to four residents, especially when the homes had to be staffed for 24 hours each day (Haycox *et al.*, 1994). Thus, it is possible that good value for money will be obtained in quite small units providing high quality of care in settings which encourage close integration in the local community.

The analysis of costs also yields the interesting suggestion that the use of qualified staff tended to produce lower overall average costs per resident in some homes. This is a lead worth following. It was also noted that efficiency in running a home was higher when home managers or officers in charge were delegated financial responsibility for the home. This also has implications for the new arrangements and the separation of enabling from providing responsibilities. Under this new arrangement, agencies will be encouraged to make each home a cost centre, partly to assist the system of making appropriate charges for residents but also partly because of the competition that is likely to emerge in the new mixed-economy approach to residential care (Darton and Wright, 1993). Enabling service providers to control their budgets will be a necessary element in the provision of efficient and effective care.

Conclusion

The research has produced many findings on the costs and quality of residential care which can guide the agencies responsible into improving the quality of lives of their residents. It has, however, concentrated heavily on the quality of the environment and process of care. There are two aspects of quality which still need to be explored in new studies. The first of these concerns the views of residents. It is a logical extension of this work to see how people with learning disabilities value the different types of home, the routines employed, their opportunities to form friendships outside as well as inside homes, and to enjoy the pursuit of recreation, amusement, occupation and employment as valued members of society. A wholly new and different methodology and set of questionnaires, measures and scales need to be developed, but without such views our knowledge of the effectiveness of care and its links with the quality of care is seriously limited.

The second avenue of discovery is concerned with relating the quality of the environment and process of care to the outcome of care in respect of the way in which they improve the social functioning, growth, development and community integration of the residents. The research has shown that over half the homes collect data on these aspects of the residents' qualities of life by using individualized planning systems. It seems perfectly reasonable to expect that the progress towards individually-set goals within these plans is a keystone in the measurement of the effectiveness of the care provided. The challenge for researchers and possibly for the staff in the Local Authority inspection units, care managers and contract compliance monitors (all now a part of the community care landscape) is to identify how these routine data can be used to show the value added to personal growth and development for the money invested in staff, buildings and services for people with learning disabilities.

Bibliography

Allen, P. T., Pahl, J. and Quine, L. (1985) *Care in the Community for People with Mental Handicaps. A study of the implications for direct care staff,* Working Paper No 2, Health Services Research Unit, University of Kent.

Arndt, S. (1981) 'A general measure of adaptive behaviour', *American Journal of Mental Deficiency,* 85, 554–6.

Audit Commission (1986) *Making a Reality of Community Care,* London: HMSO.

Avebury, Lady K. (1984) *Home Life: A code of practice for residential care,* London: Centre for Policy on Ageing.

Baker, B. L., Seltzer, G. and Seltzer, M. M. (1977) *As Close as Possible,* Boston: Little Brown.

Barton, R. (1959) *Institutional Neurosis,* Bristol: Wright.

Bjaanes, A. T. and Butler, E. W. (1974) 'Environmental variation in community care facilities for mentally retarded persons', *American Journal of Mental Deficiency,* 78, 4, 429–39.

Breyer, F. (1987) 'The specification of a hospital cost function. A comment on the recent literature', *Journal of Health Economics,* 6, 147–57.

Chartered Institute of Public Finance and Accountancy (1988a) *Personal Social Services Statistics. Actuals 1986–7,* London: CIPFA.

Chartered Institute of Public Finance and Accountancy (1988b) *Education Actuals 1986–7,* London: CIPFA.

Conroy, J. (1980) *Reliability of the Behaviour Development Survey,* Philadelphia: Temple University Development and Disabilities Center.

Conroy, J. and Bradley, V. J. (1985) *The Pennhurst Longitudinal Study: A report of five years of research and analysis,* Philadelphia: Temple University Developmental Disabilities Centre, and Boston: Human Services Research Institute.

Conroy, J. and Feinstein, C. (1986) *The Choice-Making Scale,* Philadelphia: Conroy and Feinstein Associates.

Dalgleish, M. (1983) 'Assessment of residential environments for mentally retarded adults in Britain, *Mental Retardation,* 21, 204–208.

Darton, R. A. and Wright, K. G. (1993) 'Changes in the provision of long-stay care, 1970–1990'. *Health and Social Care in the Community,* 1, 11–25.

Davies, L. (1988) 'Community care – the costs and quality', *Health Services Management Research,* 1, 3, 145–55.

Davies, L., Felce, D., Lowe, K. and de Paiva, S. (1990) *The Evaluation of NIMROD: a community based service for people with mental handicap. Revenue Costs,* Cardiff Mental Handicap in Wales – Applied Research Unit.

Department of Health (1989) *Caring for People: Community care in the next decade and beyond,* CM849, London: HMSO.

Department of Health and Social Security (1986) *SBH112D Returns for Community Provision for Mentally Handicapped People: NHS community units in England,* London: HMSO.

Department of Health and Social Security (1987a) *Residential Accommodation for the Mentally Handicapped,* Gazetteer of Local Authority Homes (RA9A), London: HMSO.

Department of Health and Social Security (1987b) *Residential Accommodation for the Mentally Handicapped,* Gazetteer of Voluntary and Private Homes (RA9B), London: DHSS.

Felce, D. (1986) 'Accommodating adults with severe and profound mental handicaps: comparative revenue costs, *Mental Handicap,* 14, 104–107.

Felce, D. and De Kock, U. (1986) 'Accommodating adults with severe and profound mental handicaps: comparative capital costs', *Mental Handicap,* 14, 26–9.

Goffman, E. (1961) *Asylums,* New York: Doubleday.

Griffiths, Sir R. (1987) *Community Care: Agenda for action,* London: HMSO.

Haycox, A., Leedham, I. and Wright, K. (1994) *Evaluating Community Care: Services for people with learning difficulties,* Buckingham: Open University Press.

Heal, L. W., Sigelman, C. K. and Sivitzky, H. N. (1980) 'Research on community residential alternatives for the mentally retarded', in Flynn, R. J. and Nitsch, K. E. (eds) *Normalization, Social Integration and Community Services,* Baltimore: University Park Press.

Heal, L. W., Wieck, C., Bruininks, R. H., Lakin, K. C. and Hill, B. C. (1988) 'Predictors of home care cost for public and community residential facilities in the United States', paper presented to the 8th meeting of the International Association for the Scientific Study of Mental Deficiency.

Jones, P. A., Conroy, J. W., Feinstein, C. S. and Lemanowicz, J. A. (1984) 'A matched comparison study of cost-effectiveness: Institutionalised and deinstitutionalised people, *Journal of the Association for Persons with Severe Handicaps,* 9, 4, 304–313.

Judge, K., Knapp, M. and Smith, J. (1986) 'The comparative costs of public and private residential homes for the elderly', in Judge, K. and Sinclair, I. (eds) *Residential Care for Elderly People,* London: HMSO.

Kind, P., Rosser, R. M. and Williams, A. (1982) 'Valuation of quality of life: Some psychometric evidence', in Jones-Lee, M. W. (ed.) *The Value of Life and Safety,* Geneva: North Holland.

King, R. D., Raynes, N. V. and Tizard, J. (1971) *Patterns of Residential Care. Sociological studies in institutions for handicapped children,* London: Routledge and Kegan Paul.

Knapp, M., Cambridge, P., Thomason, C., Beecham, J., Allen, C. and Darton, R. (1992) Care in the Community: Challenge and demonstration, Aldershot:

Ashgate.
Leonard, A. (1987) *Out of Hospital,* York: University of York.
Malin, N. (1987) 'Community care: Principles, policy and practice', in Malin, N. (ed.) *Reassessing Community Care,* Beckenham: Croom Helm.
National Development Group (1980) *Improving the Quality of Services for Mentally Handicapped People: A checklist of standards,* London: National Development Group for Mentally Handicapped People.
Nihira, K. (1976) 'Development of adaptive behaviour in the mentally retarded', in Mittler, P. (ed.) R*esearch to Practice in Mental Retardation: Vol II,* Baltimore: University Park Press.
O'Brien, J. (1987) 'A guide to personal futures planning', in Bellamy, G. T. and Wilcox, B. (eds) *A Comprehensive Guide to the Activities Catalog: An alternative curriculum for youths and adults with severe disabilities,* Baltimore: Paul H Brookes.
O'Connor, G. (1976) *Home is a Good Place,* Washington DC: American Association on Mental Deficiency.
Pratt, M. W., Luszcz, M. A. and Brown, M. E. (1979) 'Measuring dimensions of the quality of care in small community residences', *American Journal of Mental Deficiency,* 85, 2, 188–94.
Pugh, D. S., Hickson, D. J. and Hinings, C. R. (1969) 'An empirical taxonomy of structure of work organisation', *Administrative Science Quarterly,* 14, 115–26.
Raynes, N. V. (1988) *An Annotated Directory of Measures of Environmental Quality,* Manchester: University of Manchester.
Raynes, N. V. (1990) 'Shaky foundations for new structure', *Insight,* April 11, 21–2.
Raynes, N. V. and Sumpton, R. (1986) *Follow up Study of 448 People who are mentally handicapped,* Final Report to DHSS, Manchester: Department of Social Administration, University of Manchester.
Raynes, N. V. and Sumpton, R. (1987) 'Differences in the quality of residential provision for mentally handicapped people', *Psychological Medicine,* 17, 999–1008.
Raynes, N. V., Pratt, M. W. and Roses, S. (1977) 'Resident's management practice scale II', in Johnson, O. (ed.) *Test Measurement in Childhood Development II,* London: Sage.
Raynes, N. V., Pettipher, C., Shiell, A. and Wright, K. (1990) 'Keep up the small talk', *The Health Services Journal,* 2 August, 1149.
Raynes, N. V., Pettipher, C., Shiell, A. and Wright, K. (1991) 'Attitudes to clients with mental handicap', *Nursing Standard,* 5, 25–7.
Sackett, D. L. and Torrance, G. W. (1978) 'The utility of different health states as perceived by the general public', *Journal of Chronic Disease,* 31, 11, 697–704.
Selzer, G. B. (1981) 'Community residential adjustment: The relationship among environment, performance and satisfaction', *American Journal of*

Mental Deficiency, 85, 624–30.
Shiell, A. and Wright, K. (1987) *Counting the Costs of Community Care,* York: Centre for Health Economics: University of York, Occasional Paper.
Shiell, A., Wright, K., Pettipher, C. and Raynes, N. V. (1992) 'Resource management in community residential facilities for adults with learning disabilities', *Health Services Management Research,* 5, 208–15.
Social Services Inspectorate (1989) *Inspection of Day Services for People with a Mental Handicap,* London: Department of Health.
Vitaliano, D. (1987) 'On the estimation of hospital cost functions', *Journal of Health Economics,* 6, 305–18.
Wagner, G. (1988) *Residential Care: A positive choice,* London: HMSO.
Willcocks, D., Peace, S. and Kellaher, L. (1987) *Private Lives in Public Places,* London: Tavistock.
Wolfensberger, W. (1972) *The Principle of Normalisation in Human Services,* Toronto: National Institute on Mental Retardation.
Wright, K. and Haycox, A. (1985) *Costs of Alternative Forms of NHS Care for Mentally Handicapped Persons,* York: University of York, Centre for Health Economics.

Index

Italics have been used where tables are included.

activities:
   daytime *51–2*
   evenings and weekends 34, *52–3*
adult autonomy 11–12, *47*
agencies *9*, 20
   costs 82–3, 93
   management 20–29
   multi-agency homes 20, 29
   single-agency homes 20, 29
amenities:
   community *58*
   local *55*
bibliography 100–03
care:
   plans 38, 51
   practice *74*
   qualifications 91
   quality *see* qualities, of care; services
choice-making 12–14, 35–6, *47–8*, 89, 93, 95, 97
clothing and personal possessions 48
community:
   amenities 36, 93
   care 2–3, 92–4, 99
   integration 98–9
   living facilities 37, 87
   resettlement in 3
   residential provision *see* residential homes
costs:
   dependency *83*, 85, *40*
   non-residents 21
   non-staff 86
   per day *81–3*, 92
      by size *81–5*
      by type *86–7*
   per resident 98
   recurrent, non-staff 22
   regression, coefficients *90–1*
   residential homes 87, 4, 80–94, 99
   studies 98
   variations 87–94
daily routines 3, 40–1, 45, 95, 97, 99

day services 22, 29, 33, 87, 97
   elderly 34
dependency, costs *83*, 85
disabled people *40*, 96
domestic life, participation in 11, *46–7*
domiciliary health services 22–3
environment, physical 42–3, 87-8
environmental:
   measures 58–9
   quality 36–8, *60*
facilities 6, *25–9, see also* costs
   access 6–7
   declared aims *32*
   general 97
   living spaces 20
   management of principle resource 28
   respite services 33, *see also* respite care
   sizes 20, *30–31*
families and friends 15, 36, 38, *54–7,* 96
fee-income 92
financial control 63, *72–3,* 98
government policy 92
Group Homes Management Scale (GHMS) 16–17, *46*
Health Authorities 29
   community units 30
   facilities 5–6
Health, Department of, *All Wales Strategy* 1
holidays 36, *57,* 96
homeliness 38–45, 62, 97–8
hospitals 3
   size of facilities 30–1
housing associations 29
income support payments 95
individualised Programme Plans (IPPs) 36, *49–51*
individualized:
   accommodation 97
   care 45, *61,* 97, 98
   residential homes 35–6
inspection units 98–9
key workers 36, *48–9*
learning difficulties *see* learning disabilities
learning disabilities 1–2
   living 95
   services 99
   staff attitudes 68
Local Authorities:
   facilities 5–6
   homes 97, *see also* residential homes
   responsibilities 95–6
local communities 2, 96–7

management visits, staff *68–9*
meals:
   menu planning 72
   times 19, 38, *41–2, 44–5,* 97
   on wheels 34
mental handicap 69, *see also* learning disabilities
mental retardation *see* learning disabilities
money, training in use of 36, *54*
night-staff 86
non-residential 21, 33–4
non-staff expenditures 86
philosophy of care *74,* 97
private sectors 3, 35, *see also* residential homes
   facilities 5–6, 24–6, 89
      costs 21–2
qualities:
   of care 3, 87, 93, 96–9
   of environment 99
   of lives of residents 99
   of services 4, 29, *74,* 93
   variables *89–93*
      functional form 89
      list and description *88*
research staff 6
resettlement in community 3
residential care:
   see also residential homes
   elderly people 3
   objectives 1–2, 95
   quality 98
   resources 22–3
residential homes 2–3, 4, 35, 98
   accommodation 4, *43–4*
      size categories 4–5, 96
   capital values 23
   care 1–4, 95, 97
   costs *see* costs, residential homes
   facilities 87, 92
   housing stock 23, *38–9,* 96–7, 99
   lengths of stay 91, 91–2
   locations *25, 39–40*
   management 46
   occupancy rates 91
   ownership 97
   philosophy, statements of *74*
   residents *see* residents
   services 29
      costs 21
      functions 32–4
   size of living units 31

temperature 72
residents:
  age 75, 91
  behaviour *77–9, 82–3*, 93
  characteristics 4, 75–9, 91, 93
  charges 98
  impairments 77, 78
  medical needs 76–77
  paying 29
  previous homes *75–6*
  quality of life 99
  sex proportions 75
resource centres 33
respite care *32–4*, 87, 91
  children 33
routines *see* daily routines
Social Services 29, 98
staff 4, 63–74, 99
  attitudes 63
  autonomy *71*
  costs, residential care 22
  data 64
  length of time working with learning disabled *64–5*
  management visits *68–9*
  managers 63, 66
  meetings *70–1*
  monitoring 73
  morale and communication 67
  numbers 64
  organization 68
  qualified 98
  ratios 63–4
    by agencies *64*
    qualified/unqualified by agency *66*
  training 63, *66, 70*
  turnover 63, *65*
surveys:
  data sources *7–9*
  measures in questionnaire 11–21
  questionnaires 7–9
  response rates *9–10*
  introduction 4
voluntary:
  facilities 28–9
  organizations 29
  sectors 3, 20, 35
    facilities 5–6, 31
volunteers 23
World Health Organization 1